# The Wide World of Sport Programming

## Douglas M. Turco
### Illinois State University

ISBN 0-87563-665-9

Published by
STIPES PUBLISHING L.L.C.
10–12 Chester Street
Champaign, Illinois 61820

# TABLE OF CONTENTS

# CHAPTER ONE
## Basic Recreational Sport Programming

### Introduction

Sport is the most dominant influence in American popular culture. No other element of our society receives the media attention and individual consumption/participation as sport. Sport means business. *Sport, Inc.* reported the nation's Gross National Sports Product totaled over $55 billion in 1992, making it one of the 20 largest industries the United States. By the year 2000, the (GNSP) will reach 121.1 billion, an increase of 141 percent from 1990.

The levels of participation in selected recreational sports is shown in Table 1.

Table 1

### AGE PROFILE
### UNITED STATES SPORTS PARTICIPATION - 1990 *

| Sport | Total Participants (In Millions) | 7-11 | 12-17 | 18-34 | 35-54 | 55+ | Total |
|---|---|---|---|---|---|---|---|
| Baseball | 15.6 | 30.8 | 29.5 | 28.6 | 10.2 | 0.9 | 100 |
| Basketball | 25.1 | 18.5 | 31.5 | 38.1 | 11.0 | 0.9 | 100 |
| Bocce | 2.6 | 10.9 | 10.0 | 27.1 | 36.0 | 16.0 | 100 |
| Bicycling | 55.3 | 21.4 | 16.3 | 32.0 | 20.6 | 9.7 | 100 |
| Exercise Walking | 71.4 | 3.3 | 4.7 | 29.8 | 34.5 | 27.7 | 100 |
| Golf | 23.0 | 2.8 | 6.9 | 39.1 | 31.7 | 19.5 | 100 |
| In-Line Skating | 3.6 | 34.8 | 28.8 | 26.8 | 7.9 | 1.7 | 100 |
| Racquetball | 8.1 | 2.9 | 7.8 | 66.6 | 21.3 | 1.4 | 100 |
| Running | 23.8 | 11.5 | 19.2 | 44.8 | 20.3 | 4.2 | 100 |
| Skateboarding | 7.5 | 41.7 | 40.7 | 13.8 | 2.9 | 0.9 | 100 |
| Soccer | 10.9 | 42.6 | 34.3 | 17.8 | 5.0 | 0.3 | 100 |
| Softball | 20.1 | 16.6 | 19.3 | 47.3 | 15.1 | 1.7 | 100 |
| Swimming | 67.5 | 16.3 | 15.7 | 35.4 | 22.1 | 10.5 | 100 |
| Tennis | 18.4 | 7.2 | 20.0 | 47.7 | 19.4 | 5.7 | 100 |
| Volleyball | 23.2 | 7.9 | 24.6 | 49.2 | 17.0 | 1.3 | 100 |
| Football | 14.5 | 19.5 | 35.3 | 38.0 | 6.7 | 0.5 | 100 |

* Participated More Than Once
Source: National Sporting Goods Association (NSGA)

Since 1987, exercise walking has grown significantly in popularity, particularly among females (See Table 2). Other sports showing modest gains in participation since 1987 include bicycling, golf, tennis, and soccer.

## UNITED STATES SPORTS PARTICIPATION - 1991
## BY AGE

| Sport | Total Participants (In Millions) | Participants By Age | | | | |
|---|---|---|---|---|---|---|
| | | 7–11 | 12–17 | 18–34 | 35–54 | 55+ |
| Aerobic Exercise | 25.9 | 1.0 | 1.5 | 12.9 | 8.4 | 1.8 |
| Baseball | 16.5 | 5.2 | 4.8 | 4.2 | 2.0 | 0.1 |
| Basketball | 26.1 | 4.9 | 7.9 | 9.2 | 3.7 | 0.2 |
| Bicycling | 53.9 | 11.0 | 9.3 | 14.9 | 13.5 | 4.9 |
| Bocce | 2.6 | 0.3 | 0.2 | 0.7 | 1.0 | 0.4 |
| Exercise Walking | 69.5 | 2.0 | 2.8 | 19.5 | 25.2 | 16.7 |
| Football | 13.2 | 2.8 | 4.4 | 5.0 | 1.0 | 0.0 |
| Golf | 24.7 | 0.7 | 1.6 | 9.1 | 8.0 | 5.0 |
| In-Line Skating | 3.6 | 1.3 | 1.0 | 1.0 | 0.2 | 0.1 |
| Racquetball | 6.2 | 0.1 | 0.4 | 3.9 | 1.4 | 0.1 |
| Running | 22.4 | 2.2 | 4.0 | 9.4 | 2.6 | 1.0 |
| Skateboarding | 7.5 | 3.1 | 3.1 | 1.0 | 0.2 | 0.1 |
| Skiing-Alpine | 10.4 | 0.6 | 1.6 | 4.9 | 2.8 | 0.2 |
| Soccer | 9.9 | 3.7 | 3.5 | 2.0 | 0.5 | 0.0 |
| Softball | 19.6 | 2.3 | 4.2 | 8.9 | 3.7 | 0.2 |
| Swimming | 66.1 | 10.2 | 9.9 | 21.9 | 17.2 | 6.7 |
| Tennis | 16.7 | 1.0 | 2.9 | 7.5 | 4.1 | 0.7 |
| Volleyball | 22.5 | 1.7 | 5.0 | 11.1 | 4.2 | 0.2 |

Source: National Sporting Goods Association, Mt. Prospect, IL, *Sports Participation in 1991, Series I.*
*Participated More Than Once
Source: National Sporting Goods Association (NSGA)

## UNITED STATES PARTICIPATION IN SPORT ACTIVITIES, 1991
## BY GENDER

| | MALE | | FEMALE | | TOTAL |
|---|---|---|---|---|---|
| | N | Percent | N | Percent | N |
| Aerobic Exercise | 4.4 | 16.9% | 21.4 | 73.1% | 25.9 |
| Baseball | 13.6 | 82.4 | 2.9 | 17.6 | 16.5 |
| Basketball | 19.1 | 73.2 | 7.0 | 26.8 | 26.1 |
| Bicycle Riding | 26.9 | 49.9 | 27.0 | 50.1 | 53.9 |
| Bowling | 21.0 | 52.1 | 19.3 | 47.9 | 40.3 |
| Fishing | 37.1 | 69.2 | 16.5 | 30.8 | 53.6 |
| Football | 11.7 | 88.6 | 1.6 | 11.4 | 13.2 |
| Golf | 18.6 | 75.3 | 6.1 | 24.7 | 24.7 |
| Racquetball | 4.7 | 75.8 | 1.5 | 24.2 | 6.2 |
| Running | 13.1 | 58.4 | 9.3 | 41.6 | 22.4 |
| Alpine Skiing | 6.0 | 57.7 | 4.4 | 42.3 | 10.4 |
| X-country Skiing | 2.0 | 46.5 | 2.3 | 53.5 | 4.3 |
| Soccer | 6.6 | 66.7 | 3.3 | 33.3 | 9.9 |
| Softball | 11.8 | 60.2 | 7.8 | 39.8 | 19.6 |
| Swimming | 30.8 | 46.5 | 35.3 | 53.5 | 66.1 |
| Tennis | 9.2 | 55.1 | 7.5 | 44.9 | 16.7 |
| Exercise Walking | 24.7 | 35.5 | 44.8 | 64.5 | 69.5 |
| Volleyball | 11.4 | 50.7 | 11.0 | 49.3 | 22.5 |

Source: National Sporting Goods Association, Mt. Prospect, IL, *Sports Participation in 1991, Series I.*

## UNITED STATES PARTICIPATION IN SPORT ACTIVITIES, 1991 BY INCOME

### HOUSEHOLD INCOME IN DOLLARS

|  | Under 15,000 | 15,000– 24,999 | 25,000– 34,999 | 35,000– 49,999 | 50,000– 74,999 | 75,000 and over |
|---|---|---|---|---|---|---|
| Aerobic Ex. | 14.6% | 12.2% | 16.3% | 21.0% | 23.5% | 12.3% |
| Basketball | 13.2 | 14.7 | 17.5 | 20.5 | 23.2 | 10.8 |
| Bicycling | 16.4 | 13.6 | 16.4 | 19.1 | 23.2 | 11.2 |
| Golf | 9.4 | 12.0 | 14.6 | 18.1 | 29.6 | 16.1 |
| Running | 15.9 | 12.2 | 15.5 | 18.0 | 25.5 | 13.1 |
| Alpine Skiing | 6.3 | 6.4 | 12.4 | 16.6 | 36.9 | 21.7 |
| Soccer | 10.0 | 11.8 | 16.9 | 19.7 | 29.0 | 12.6 |
| Swimming | 15.3 | 12.4 | 15.9 | 21.0 | 23.6 | 11.7 |
| Tennis | 10.6 | 10.3 | 16.6 | 17.3 | 27.4 | 17.8 |
| Walking | 17.8 | 15.7 | 16.2 | 19.2 | 21.6 | 9.4 |
| Volleyball | 15.4 | 15.7 | 17.2 | 23.7 | 19.7 | 8.1 |

Source: National Sporting Goods Association, Mt. Prospect, IL, *Sports Participation in 1991, Series I.*

## TRENDS IN SPORTS PARTICIPATION 1987–1990
### In Millions of Participants

| SPORT | MALES | | | | FEMALES | | | |
|---|---|---|---|---|---|---|---|---|
|  | 1987 | 1988 | 1989 | 1990 | 1987 | 1988 | 1989 | 1990 |
| Swimming | 31.2 | 32.4 | 33.2 | 31.6 | 34.8 | 38.7 | 37.3 | 35.9 |
| Bicycling | 25.9 | 26.1 | 28.4 | 28.1 | 27.4 | 27.8 | 28.6 | 27.1 |
| Exercise Walking | 20.6 | 21.0 | 23.7 | 25.1 | 37.5 | 41.3 | 42.9 | 46.3 |
| Bowling | 19.7 | 19.1 | 21.3 | 20.9 | 20.4 | 18.7 | 19.6 | 19.2 |
| Basketball | 18.0 | 16.5 | 19.1 | 18.9 | 7.1 | 6.6 | 7.1 | 7.4 |
| Golf | 15.2 | 17.2 | 17.4 | 17.3 | 5.0 | 5.5 | 5.7 | 5.7 |
| Running | 14.2 | 13.4 | 14.5 | 13.0 | 10.6 | 9.6 | 10.3 | 10.8 |
| Baseball | 12.1 | 10.8 | 12.1 | 12.6 | 3.1 | 2.5 | 3.3 | 3.0 |
| Football | 12.9 | 10.8 | 12.8 | 12.4 | 2.1 | 1.5 | 1.9 | 2.0 |
| Softball | 12.9 | 12.1 | 13.4 | 11.6 | 8.7 | 8.5 | 8.7 | 8.5 |
| Volleyball | 11.7 | 10.5 | 13.0 | 11.2 | 11.9 | 11.5 | 12.1 | 12.0 |
| Tennis | 9.3 | 9.7 | 10.4 | 10.3 | 7.6 | 7.6 | 8.4 | 8.1 |
| Soccer | 6.2 | 5.5 | 7.5 | 7.0 | 3.7 | 3.2 | 3.7 | 3.9 |
| Racquetball | 5.6 | 6.5 | 6.2 | 6.0 | 2.3 | 2.9 | 2.1 | 2.1 |
| Skateboarding | 5.1 | 5.6 | 5.8 | 6.1 | 1.9 | 1.7 | 1.6 | 1.4 |
| X-C Skiing | 2.5 | 2.8 | 2.4 | 2.6 | 2.5 | 2.9 | 2.5 | 2.5 |
| Ice Hockey | 1.1 | 1.6 | 1.3 | 1.7 | 0.1 | 0.2 | 0.2 | 0.2 |

*Participated More Than Once
Source: National Sporting Goods Association (NSGA)

## Sport Agencies

As participation has grown in recreational, amateur and professional sport as well as fitness-related activities, the sport industry has responded to the demand with enhanced programs and opportunities for individuals and groups.

There are three major classifications of community sport providers. Each of these classifications includes two or more sport sub-categories that have similar objectives and provide like services but serve a different target market or occur in a different setting. These classifications can be further delineated by profit motive, that is, having a profit or nonprofit orientation.

### SPORT PROVIDERS

1. Local settings include nonprofit agencies that develop, implement and mange recreational sports programs, activities or facilities to meet the needs of agency members or citizens of designated governmental units (e.g., town, city, district, county).
    o Municipal Recreation and Parks Departments
    o Voluntary Organizations (i.e., YM/YWCA, Boys Club, etc.)
    o Sport Clubs/Organizations (i.e., Little League, Youth Soccer, etc.)

2. Organizations that provide opportunities for sport and fitness participation through facilities and programs for members, including:
    o Commercial Recreation Enterprises
        Fitness Centers    Bowling Lanes
        Racquet Clubs    Golf Country Clubs
        Sport Centers
    o Corporate and company sport and fitness programs
    o Colleges and Universities Recreational Sport Programs (Intramurals) and Sport Clubs

3. Organizations that provide management of sporting events, athletes and/or spectator consumption, such as:
    o College and University Athletic Departments
    o Sport Management Services
    o Professional Sport
    o Amateur Athletic Organizations

## Sport Formats

Sport has many forms and is defined in several categories (See Table 3). Sport may be classified as an individual activity to be carried out without a team, partner or opponent. Dual sports are those requiring at least two persons to participate. Activities such as tennis, racquetball, and wrestling are dual sports. Team sports require a group of people to implement the activity. Team sports include:

4

## SPORT PROGRAM FORMATS

| Sport | Class | Workshop | Special Event | Drop-In | Competition | Club |
|-------|-------|----------|---------------|---------|-------------|------|
| Golf | Beginning Lessons | Turf Management | Pro-Am | Public Golf | City Championships | Ladies of Golf |
| Softball | T-Ball Instructions | Youth Coaches' Clinic | All-Star Tournament | Diamonds | Fast-Pitch Tournament | Fast-Pitch Club |
| Swimming | Water Aerobics | Pool Maintenance Seminar | Sychorized Swimming Performance | Open Swim | Swim Meet | Masters Swim Club |
| Tennis | Advanced Tennis | Serving Workshop | Pro Exhibition Match | Tennis Courts | Tennis Ladder | Early Birds |
| Volleyball | Power Volleyball Lessons | Officials' Workshop | Pro-Beach Voleyball Championships | Sand Courts | Volleyball Tournament | Volleyball Club |

5

Table 3
Partial List of Individual, Dual and Team Sports

| Individual Sports | Dual Sports | Team Sports |
|---|---|---|
| Golf | Tennis | Hockey |
| Weight Lifting | Boxing | Soccer |
| Bowling | Wrestling | Basketball |
| Track and Field | Racquetball | Softball |
| Swimming | Table Tennis | Volleyball |
| Skiing | | Walleyball |
| Gymnastics | | Baseball |
| Skating | | Football |
| Triathlon | | Rugby |

Dual sports offer the opportunity for integrating men and women in coed or co-rec participation. Dual sports can play a part in the stability of male/female and same gender relationships. Couples are able to schedule a matches 'til death do they part', providing that a balance of skill and interest is maintained.

A primary value of team play is the opportunity for participants to achieve a sense of belonging. Even in defeat there is commonality of emotions, a sense of empathy and found.

## Goal Structure

Sheffield (1984) advocates categorizing recreational activities based on goal structure. Based on the participant's goal structure, activities are classified as competitive, individual, and cooperative. In the competitive goal structure, in order for one entry to achieve her goal, other entries must be prevented from achieving theirs. The individual goal structure allows each individual to achieve their goal; all or some of the participants may achieve their goal; the individual's goal is not related to any other participant's goal. Cooperative structure can only be accomplished when all participants accomplish their individual goals (See Table 5).

In a competitive sport format, a participant's performance is measured in relation to the performance of another, or in terms of established standards of performance. An individual may compete against herself or himself so that s/he may measure her or his level of performance and train toward further improvement of performance. An individual may compete against an opponent - either head-to-head or in a contest, which is a comparison of performances where opponents do not interfere with the performance of each other.

As a participant moves from an informal play activity to a structured sport or athletics, several changes in attitude and behavior are noticeable. Edwards (1974: 59) contends the following occurs:

6

1. Activity becomes less subject to individual perogative, with spontaneity diminished.

2. Formal rules and structural role and position relationships and responsibilities with the activity assume predominance.

3. Separation from the rigors and pressures of daily life becomes less prevalent.

4. Individual liability and responsibility for the quality and character of behavior during the course of the activity is heightened.

5. The relevance of the outcome of the activity and the individual's role in it extends to groups and collectivities that do not directly participate in the act.

6. Goals become diverse, complex, and more related to values emanating from outside the context of the activity.

7. The activity consumes a greater proportion of the indiviual's time and attention due to the need for preparation and the degree of seriousness involved in the act.

8. The emphasis on physical and mental extension beyond the limits of refreshness or interest in the act assumes increasing dominance.

## Basic Sport Programming

Recreational sports programs offer unique planning considerations in comparison to a typical community recreation class, such as beginning guitar lessons. Human and physical resources must be carefully coordinated. The safety of the sports participants is of the utmost importance, necessitating a thorough risk management plan. Specific rules and regulations often govern the nature of the sports program. For example, a triathlon championship race (typically combining swimming, running and bicycling) must be sanctioned by TriFed, the sports official body, to ensure that race distances meet previously established standards, thereby qualifying race winners for advanced competitions (i.e., Ironman World Triathlon Championships) Few basic program planning texts have addressed these characteristics inherent to sports programming.

Most park and recreation students and professionals have learned the basic steps in program planning through college/university courses, continuing educational sessions, or by discovery through trial and error. Program planning has been the subject of numerous books by several scholars - each offering a model for the planning process (Kraus, 1989; Patterson, 1987; Farrel & Lundegren, 1978; Rossman, 1989; Corbin and Williams, 1987; Bannon, 1976). While their planning models differ in

Sport Program Planning Cycle

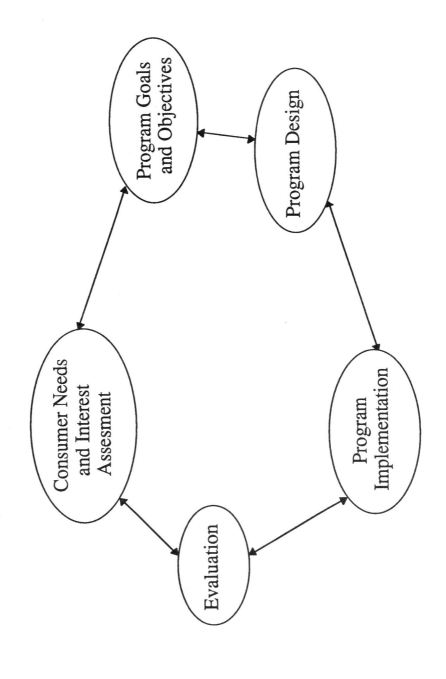

design, they conceptually agree on the following five program planning steps: (1) Needs and interests assessment, (2) determining objectives, (3) program design, (4) implementation, and (5) evaluation. These steps are part of a continuous programming process, as illustrated in Figure 1.

Why should the programmer adhere to the steps in the planning process? Today, recreational sports programs must be purposeful and goal orientated. Local government administrators, officials and consumers are requiring that public agencies become more accountable for their actions and expenditures. Often, department programs are subject to careful evaluation and documentation of outcomes to justify a program's resource allocation. Further, the quality of services offered to the consumer is dependent on proper planning, and ultimately, the success and reputation of the agency. This unit is intended to serve as an introduction to the basics of recreational sports programming and to emphasize the importance of following the steps involved in the planning process.

## Step One - Needs and Interests Assessment

Consumer preferences define the sports program planning task. Various methods may be employed to determine the recreational sports needs and interests of a community. The professional judgement of the park and recreation department programmer is an important method in determining constituent need. The recreational sport manager is aware of current trends in the field and able to gauge the constituency's pulse through observation and direct communication with the citizenry. Utilizing public hearings, focus groups and citizen advisory councils are other important need assessment techniques. Mail or telephone surveys of the population may also be conducted. Sometimes, the personal and/or political interests of high ranking government officials becomes a factor in determining program need. For example, if the son or daughter of a city councilor is interested in playing youth soccer, the official may strongly advocate the establishment of a youth soccer program, including allocating department funds and staff time to develop such a program.

In assessing community needs and interests, park and recreation professionals should also gather comprehensive data about the available facilities and programs sponsored by other agencies in different sections of the community. Based on gathered information and with a knowledge of the recreation needs and interests of the citizens, it is possible to effectively plan programs that meet citizen needs. Below are several methods of assessing consumer needs and interests along with their respective advantages and disadvantages.

## Step Two - Determining Goals and Objectives

Recreational sport planners are often guilty of implementing activities without considering what they want to accomplish by them. Programs without clearly defined objectives are virtually impossible to evaluate. Goals and objectives both represent outcomes that an organization and participants seek to achieve. In recreation literature, the two terms often seem interchangeable. However, their meanings are quite different. Goals are broad statements of purpose that help shape a department's philosophy in terms of major outcomes to be achieved (Kraus, 1985, 128). Goals can be further broken down into objectives which specify short-term expectations. Objectives are specific, measurable program outcomes to be achieved within a set period of time. Objectives can be easily adjusted to meet the needs and interests of participants and the sponsoring organization. Frequently each goal has several objectives attached to it.

There are two types of objectives that a program planner develops - *operational objectives* and *performance objectives*. Operational objectives are the methods used to conduct the program and typically include such factors as leadership, facilities and administration. Performance objectives are concerned with the program outcomes. "Performance objectives describe the behavior or attitude that the program's target constituency should demonstrate at its conclusion - some skill, attitude, or knowledge they did not have before (Russell, 1982: 113)." Examples of operational and performance objectives for an outdoor swim meet for older adults are in Figure 2.

---

### FIGURE 2

**Activity:** Swimming Competition for the Older Adults

> **Operational Objective** - The program will maintain the contracted services of two certified water safety instructors for the duration of the program.

> **Performance Objective** - At the conclusion of the event, each participant will be able to accurately demonstrate the freestyle flip-turn for swim competition.

---

A checklist with detailed time tables indicating when the program's operational objectives should be completed must be developed at the conclusion of this stage. Table 6 provides a example of a partial checklist for the "SuperSwimII" aquatics program.

TABLE 6

SuperSwim II
Program Planning Checklist

**Actual Date of**
**Completed Task**                                       **Task**

_____Secure contract with water safety instructors to teach course by June 1.

_____Mail course registration materials to past participants, senior club members by June 24.

_____Create and release PSA's and news articles promoting the activity to local media agencies by June 31.

_____Event registration begins.

_____Conduct race orientation meeting July 13.

_____Conduct activity/instructor evaluation by July 28.

_____Hold activity/instructor evaluation review meeting by July 29.


## Step Three - Program Design

How can the previously stated objectives best be met? This question should be asked throughout Stage Three of the planning process. Programs are the actions required to achieve stated objectives. Creative thinking is necessary for generating program solutions. Identify alternative/innovative ways a program can meet the consumer's needs and interests.

Selecting the "right" program alternative is generally based on its feasibility, practicality, and cost-effectiveness. As a public servant, the recreation program planner should not impose her/his own preferences of what is good or bad. Factors that must be considered when selecting a program include: Amount of human and financial resources required and available, dates, times, and program location. Typically, financial resources are in the form of appropriations from the park and recreation department account, user fees, and sponsor contributions. Basic program expenditures include staff salary and wages, contract service costs, and purchases for equipment and supplies. Final program plans are often a compromise between what the planner ideally wants to achieve and the financial resource limitations and political realities within the department. However, seek to develop programs of the highest quality. The City of Cookeville, Tennessee Department of Parks and Recreation guarantees its customers satisfaction or their money back (Chambers, 1990). Only a confident park and recreation department with well-planned programs can make this claim.

## Step Four - Implementation

This stage involves a number of specific tasks, including: (1) designating personnel to leadership and supervisory positions, (2) developing a program promotional plan, (3) preparing a risk management plan to prevent accidents and maintain a safe recreation environment (Kraus, p. 241).

### Personnel

Staff and/or volunteers must be scheduled. Depending on the nature of the activity, there may or may not be paid personnel assigned to leadership and supervisory positions. Rather than using city employees to provide leisure services, many park and recreation departments are entering into contractual arrangements with external service providers. Bretting and Turco (1990) determined that 82 percent of large city park and recreation departments (population over 100,000) utilize contract service arrangements for concessions, class instruction, entertainment, lifeguarding, officiating, and maintenance. Bartling (1980) developed a handbook to assist recreation professionals in managing contractual agreements with external service providers.

Registration procedures must also be finalized. Determine registration procedures (in-person, mail, telephone, fax, etc.), methods of payment (i.e., installment, deposit, credit card, cash, etc.) deadlines, class size - maximum, minimum, pricing. The price to participate in a recreation program is based on several factors such as the program's objectives, estimated revenues, and expenditures.

### Promotional Planning

Before most programs are put into action, they must be publicized to attract participants. Promotional efforts may be carried out a number of ways, including: Press releases, feature articles, community calendar, announcements on the local cable television access channel, public service announcements, direct mail to a targeted audience and/or past participants, seasonal program brochures, flyers, media advertisements, word-of-mouth, and posters. Financial resource availability and consumer demand usually dictates which, if any, of these promotional methods will be employed. Chapter Two of this text is devoted to marketing sports programs and more thoroughly addresses the area of promotional planning.

### Risk Management

Many park and recreation departments have created comprehensive risk management plans that analyze and interpret the risks inherent to an activity and develop methods for minimizing accidents. To minimize the risks in a program, planners should consider the following:

1. Select appropriate activities for the program's targeted population

**Miller Genuine Draft**

**SHOOT THE BULL**
3 ON 3 CLASSIC

# DEADLINE TO REGISTER IS JULY 15

OR sign up by May 6 and take advantage of our special Early Bull offer and receive a Chicago Bulls Championship video! *(for team captains only)*

☐ Please find enclosed my payment of $100 ☐ Please find enclosed my payment of $125 for the Chicago Tribune Corporate Challenge

OFFICE USE ONLY:

*Take Time for Fun!*

TEAM #:
DATE:
CK OR MO #:
AMOUNT:

## TEAM NAME _____ (PLEASE PRINT)

| CAPTAIN ☐ M ☐ F | PLAYER #2 ☐ M ☐ F | PLAYER #3 ☐ M ☐ F | PLAYER #4 *(optional)* ☐ M ☐ F |
|---|---|---|---|
| Name _____ | Name _____ | Name _____ | Name _____ |
| Address _____ | Address _____ | Address _____ | Address _____ |
| City _____ State ___ Zip ___ | City _____ State ___ Zip ___ | City _____ State ___ Zip ___ | City _____ State ___ Zip ___ |
| Day Phone (___) ___ | Day Phone (___) ___ | Day Phone (___) ___ | Day Phone (___) ___ |
| Evening Phone (___) ___ | Evening Phone (___) ___ | Evening Phone (___) ___ | Evening Phone (___) ___ |

**Experience** *(Please check your highest playing level)* [for each player]

☐ Pro Team:
☐ Mjr. College: ☐ Div I ☐ Div II
☐ Sm. College: ☐ Div III/NAIA ☐ Jr. College
☐ High School
☐ Rec. League/Playground
☐ College Intramurals
☐ Junior High
☐ Wheelchair
☐ No experience

On average, how many times do you play a week?
☐ 1 ☐ 2 ☐ 3 ☐ 4 ☐ 5+
Age ___ Height ___ Weight ___

PLAYER'S SIGNATURE*

PARENT'S OR GUARDIAN'S SIGNATURE*
(Required if player is under 18 years old)

A $100/$125 non-refundable entry fee must accompany your registration form. Make check or money order payable in full to the Chicago Bulls.
**We must receive on or before July 15, 1994.**

*My signature indicates that I have read, understand and agree to sections 8, 9 and 10 of the Official SHOOT-THE-BULL™ Registration Rules that are listed above on this form.

**Mail completed form with your *non-refundable* full payment to:**
Chicago Bulls
980 North Michigan Ave., Suite 1600, Chicago, IL 60611-4501
Attn: SHOOT-THE-BULL™
or FAX to (312)943-6739 *(when paying by credit card only)*

For credit card payment only:
☐ Visa ☐ MasterCard ☐ Discover
Acct. No. _____ Exp. Date ___
Name (PLEASE PRINT) _____ Day Phone (___) ___

THE TEAM'S AVERAGE AGE, PLAYING EXPERIENCE, HEIGHT AND WEIGHT WILL DETERMINE THE DIVISION IN WHICH THE TEAM WILL COMPETE. LARGE DISCREPANCIES ARE DISCOURAGED. CO-ED TEAMS ARE ALSO DISCOURAGED.

13

## REGISTRATION RULES

1. Official SHOOT-THE-BULL™ registration forms can also be found in the Tuesday and Sunday Chicago Tribune and at all Sportmart locations.

2. Sportmart is the official SHOOT-THE-BULL™ walk-in registration site effective April 9 - July 7. When your team registers at Sportmart, each team member will receive a coupon good for $5 off any regularly priced LA Tech shoe, the official shoe of SHOOT-THE-BULL™.

3. Registration by mail: $100 or $125 non-refundable team entry fee must accompany the completed registration form. However, if you must drive, limited parking is available at the Monroe Street parking garage located at 350 East Monroe Street. Make check or money order payable to the Chicago Bulls or include your credit card information. Faxes are accepted.

4. Each player must a) print his/her name, address and phone number; b) complete the highest level of playing experience attained; and c) sign his/her name. Incomplete registration forms will not be accepted.

5. Team captain or designee must return registration form on or before Friday, July 15. After the July 15 deadline, no additions, changes or deletions will be accepted.

6. Each team captain will receive a confirmation letter confirming receipt of team's payment and registration.

7. We reserve the right to check players' age, height, weight and playing experience. Use of inaccurate information is grounds for disqualification of the entire team. Players must carry personal identification.

### ATTENTION PLAYERS:

Rules 8, 9 and 10 refer to conditions which require your agreement for your participation in the tournament.

8. There are inherent risks associated with my participation in the tournament and its related activities. I agree to release and discharge the Chicago Professional Sports Limited Partnership, NBA Properties Inc., Miller Brewing Company, other event sponsors, event charities and event organizers, their affiliated companies and organizations, and their officers, partners, owners, employees and directors (collectively known as the "SHOOT-THE-BULL™ Personnel") from all actions, suits and demands whatsoever in law or in equity, including but not limited to those relating to the risk of loss of personal property by theft or otherwise.

9. I hereby grant full permission to any and all of the SHOOT-THE-BULL™ Personnel to use any and all registration information, and to take or use photographs, make or use motion pictures, recordings, or any other record of this event for any publicity, promotional, advertising, trade or commercial purposes, without the need to pay me any fee.

10. Player eligibility varies for NCAA, collegiate sports and local school districts. SHOOT-THE-BULL™ is not responsible for determining each player's eligibility. Before registering, contact your coach or athletic director and ask how your eligibility would be affected, if at all, by registering for SHOOT-THE-BULL™.


## HELPFUL HINTS

### RAPID TRANSIT

The tournament site is easily accessible by CTA and Metra. For information on times, routes and fares, call RTA Travel Information Center at (312)836-7000 or (708)836-7000.

We encourage you to take public transportation. However, if you must drive, limited parking is available at the Monroe Street parking garage located at 350 East Monroe Street. Rates are $5 per day.

### FIRST AID

Members of the department of Orthopedic Surgery and other medical personnel from Northwestern Memorial Hospital will be on site to attend to any minor injuries. Medical supplies are donated by Northwestern Memorial Hospital.


## REMINDABULLS

Who: Miller Genuine Draft and the Chicago Bulls in conjunction with the Chicago Tribune, Coca-Cola, Sportmart/LA Tech, Salem Sportswear and Chrysler/Plymouth . . . .

What: . . . present the sixth annual SHOOT-THE-BULL 3 on 3 Classic." The tournament is open to anyone age 14 and older. Teams will be scheduled into more than 140 divisions with other teams of comparable age, height, weight and playing experience. Every team is guaranteed at least two games . . .

Where: . . . in Chicago's Grant Park at Congress Parkway and Columbus Drive . . .

When: . . . on Saturday, July 30 and Sunday, July 31. Need to know when and where to show up on Saturday? Refer to your scheduling booklet which will be distributed at the Registration Party on Friday, July 29. At least one team member must attend. No exceptions . . .

Why: . . . for charity. A majority of team fees will benefit CharitaBulls® and Illinois Special Olympics.


## GENERAL TOURNAMENT RULES

A complete list of all game rules and regulations will appear in the official SHOOT-THE-BULL™ program.

1. Games are played to 20 points or 25 minutes; whichever comes first.

2. Baskets made are 1 point; baskets made outside the 2-point line are worth 2 points.

3. Players call their own fouls. Court monitors will keep score and time and ensure that the games run smoothly.

4. Monitors will check in players with player ID bracelets on the wrist only. NO BRACELET, NO PLAY!

5. Flagrant fouls or continuous misconduct at the monitor's discretion will result in forfeiture and dismissal from the tournament.

6. In the event of inclement weather, we reserve the right to do one or more of the following:
- move games to other courts;
- reduce the number of points needed to win and cancel games in the consolation bracket;
- change format from double to single elimination;
- cancel the event in which case FULL OR PARTIAL REFUNDS WILL NOT BE GIVEN. However, every reasonable effort will be made to keep the tournament going.

## CATEGORIES

— Professional     — Age 50+
— Major College    — Age 40-49
— Small College    — Age 21-39
— Corporate Challenge   — Age 17-20
— Wheelchair     — Age 14-16

— The scheduling process is a function of the total number of teams registered in the tournament. We reserve the right to move teams accordingly to fill a computer-ranked 16 team division.

— The team's average age, playing experience, height and weight determine the division in which the team will compete. However, the ranking method may differ among categories and is at the sole discretion of the SHOOT-THE-BULL™ staff.

# HOOP THERE IT IS!

Need a quick fix for winter's discontent? ... Take advantage of the city's parks and outdoor basketball courts ... Recruit your coworkers for a competitive (but friendly) contest ... Or, better yet, get ready for Chicago's largest hoopfest, the Miller Genuine Draft SHOOT-THE-BULL 3 on 3 Classic.

The event will be held in Chicago's Grant Park on Saturday, July 30 and Sunday, July 31. It's what you have been waiting for. And now while it's on your mind, sign up today to secure your spot for this basketball bonanza. More than 2,300 teams are expected to come out and fulfill their court of dreams on 200 baskets lining Columbus Drive.

**Everyone is invited — from the recreational to the serious, ages 14 and older.** Men, women and kids' divisions are composed of 16 computer-ranked teams offering players competitively matched games. Winners and runners-up will receive special trophies and prizes, including an official tournament basketball from Wilson Sporting Goods.* Tournament highlights include the Men's and Women's Final Four at Center Court presented by Miller Genuine Draft, with winners qualifying for the 1994 SHOOT-THE-BULL™ Finals. The 1994 Champions are invited to show their stuff at a Hoop-It-Up Regional event, compliments of Southwest Airlines. (Exact date and place to be determined.)

The real winners of SHOOT-THE-BULL™ are CharitaBulls,® the Bulls charity organization, and Illinois Special Olympics, our main provider of volunteers. Over the past five years, more than $575,000 has been donated. By participating in this tournament, you can help CharitaBulls® help the Chicago Park District renovate and restore outdoor basketball courts. Monies raised also provide year-round sports training and athletic competition for all children and adults with mental retardation. If you're not up to playing in the tournament, help us help these charities by joining our team of volunteers. To sign up, call the SHOOT-THE-BULL™ Volunteer Coordinator at Illinois Special Olympics at (708)955-3620 or the Bulls' Kelly Taylor at (312)943-5800 ext. 130.

*Corporate Challenges only.

---

# Chicago Tribune CORPORATE CHALLENGE

Replace those spreadsheets with scoresheets and enter the Chicago Tribune Corporate Challenge. Similar to other divisions, teams are matched according to age, height, weight and playing experience. In addition to receiving the official SHOOT-THE-BULL™ player gift, challengers will receive a Chicago Tribune Corporate Challenge T-shirt and a team photo opportunity on site. Test who's best in corporate basketball and sign up today. **To enter, simply check the appropriate box included on the player registration form and send along with your $125 payment.**

# SPECIAL EVENTS & CONTESTS

Don't forget to get a head start on the weekend and pick up your **essential** registration packet and gifts at the Hyatt Regency Chicago on Friday, July 29 from 4:00 to 8:00pm. The party will feature plenty of food, fun and SHOOT-THE-BULL™ merchandise, so bring your friends and family. **However, it is mandatory that at least one member of your team attend as there will be no on-site registration in Grant Park.**

As the official SHOOT-THE-BULL™ hotel, the Hyatt Regency invites participants to stay for just $88 per night for a single or double room. Refer to the enclosed Hyatt registration card for more information or call the Hyatt at (312)565-1234 to reserve your room today. Please note that this special offer is subject to availability.

 **CELEBRITY CHALLENGE**

See your favorite media personalities battle it out on center court on Saturday. Check schedule of events for exact time.

**WGCI $250,000 SHOT**

Feel like trying your luck at winning a quarter of a million dollars? The WGCI $250,000 3/4 court shot will take place at Center Court on Saturday, so don't miss out. Call WGCI at (312)427-4800 for more information on how you can qualify.

The official sports radio station of the 1994 SHOOT-THE-BULL:

WMVP Chicago's New Sports Leader

---

 **CHICAGO BULLS SLAM DUNK**

Men, women and kids are all invited to show their stuff in the Chicago Bulls Slam Dunk contest. Men's and women's slam dunk is just a $5 donation to charity. There is no charge for the kids' slam dunk (height limitations apply). **Please note that kids are randomly selected on site. No pre-registration is necessary.**

CHRYSLER Plymouth **3-POINT SHOT**

Driving down the lane won't get you points in this contest, but going the distance will. Challenge yourself and test your long-range shooting. There are divisions for men, women and kids 14 and older. The entry fee is only a $3 donation to charity.

SALEM **SHOOTOUT**

Be the hot shot and shoot from designated spots on the court. For just a $2 donation to charity, men, women and kids are all invited to take their best shot in this timed, individual contest.

Save your quarters for the **Pop-A-Shot™** contest. For just 50¢, you can try your hand at establishing a streak. Qualifying rounds are on Friday night of the annual SHOOT-THE-BULL™ Registration Party.

**Please note:** Participation in the above contests is not limited to registered SHOOT-THE-BULL™ players. To enter, simply show up at the contest court ticket tent. Contests are scheduled throughout the day on Saturday and Sunday. Please listen for announcements and updates on the public address system. A complete list of contest rules will appear in the official SHOOT-THE-BULL™ program. Category winners and runners-up will receive special prizes and gifts.

SPORTMART / LA TECH **KIDS' CAMP**

Come see some of the NBA's best give kids pointers on the basics of basketball. The clinic will be held on Saturday and Sunday at Center Court. Kids will be randomly selected on site and will receive special gifts for participating. No pre-registration is necessary.

Coca-Cola **KIDS' FINAL FOUR**

For the second consecutive year, top teams in the 14-16 age bracket will be showcased on Sunday at Center Court. Be sure to check the schedule of events for the exact time of this exciting contest.

**Please note:** In order to qualify, a minimum of 64 teams must be registered in this age bracket.

2. Ensure that the facilities and equipment are appropriate to the activity and the population.

3. Include written procedures in the event of an emergency.

4. Transfer the risk to another agent (i.e., liability insurance policy).

5. Adequate and qualified supervision must be utilized.

A total risk management plan should include the following key elements: Highly qualified leadership and carefully designed safety policies; explaining hazards to participants; obtaining their consent; and adequate preparations, including inspection of equipment and supplies. See Chapter Nine for additional discussion concerning risk management of sports programs.

## Step Five - Evaluation

Activity evaluations are often the most neglected aspect of the recreation program planning process. Written evaluations and final program reports, if properly conducted, offer a wealth of information in planning an activity again and therefore should not be overlooked. Through this process the programmer can avoid future mistakes by knowing what the past mistakes were. Evaluation should be used to determine program response, eliminate safety hazards, and as a primary method of quality control.

Prior to conducting an evaluation of the sport program, several basic questions should be asked and answered:

1. Why is an evaluation necessary?

2. Who is the evaluation for? What questions do they need answered? What will they do with the information from the evaluation?

3. How will the evaluation be conducted?

4. What questions should the evaluation address?

5. What resources are needed to conduct the evaluation?

6. What information will be gathered?

7. How will the information be gathered?

8. How will the information be analyzed?

9. How will evaluation findings be reported?

10. Do we have the human and financial resources to evaluate our sport service? Can we afford not to evaluate?

Some considerations in evaluating recreational sport programs include the following:

## Customer Satisfaction
Were participants and spectators satisfied with their experience? If not, why?
Did the quality of our services match the expectations of our customers?
Are customers likely to consumer our services in the future?
What could be done, if anything, to improve the quality of our services?

## Personnel
Did officials maintain control of the games?
Were the officials knowledgeable about the rules?
Did they start play on time?
Were league management personnel available when needed?

## Scheduling
How did spectators find out about this sport service?
Were teams in the league well matched according to their ability?
Were there too many games within the league?
Was the length of time to complete the league too long?
Was the minimum roster size for league teams adequate to minimize match forfeits?


It is advised to employ a variety of methods in the evaluation process. Conduct a participant survey through personal interviews, use customer comments cards and formal written evaluations, or both. Consider video taping the program. This technique will provide a visual reference of the program's various components, and will serve as a form of promotion if the event is implemented again. The personal observations of the program planner are also extremely useful in evaluating the activity. Conduct a post-program meeting with those involved (i.e., planning committee members, instructors, participants, etc.) and ask for oral and written recommendations and/or suggestions for improvement.

Questionnaires should feature a two dimensional approach to evaluate customers' perceptions of service quality. The first dimension should ascertain the importance customers place on certain service attributes or characteristics (i.e., cleanliness of the facility, courteous staff, quality of instruction, etc.). The second dimension should measure the customer's perception of the quality of service delivery.

In evaluating annual sporting events, information from detailed nonresident participant expenditure surveys are useful in securing resources from sponsors for next year's event. Further, an economic impact assessment may reveal a return on the municipality's budget investment in the form of tax dollars generated as a result of the event. Market information such as the town where the visitor is from, how visitors heard about the event, and visitor demographic information may also be determined through this evaluation technique. The methodology for conducting an economic impact assessment is presented in Chapter 10.

## Summary

No other element of our society receives the media attention and individual consumption/participation as sport. The nation's Gross National Sports Product (GNSP) totaled $47.2 billion in 1986, making it the 25th largest industry the United States. By the year 2000, the (GNSP) will reach 121.1 billion, an increase of 141 percent from 1990.

As participation has grown in recreational, amateur and professional sport as well as fitness-related activities, the sport industry has responded to the demand with enhanced programs and opportunities for individuals and groups.

There are five basic steps to the sport program planning process: (1) Needs and interests assessment, (2) determining objectives, (3) program design, (4) implementation, and (5) evaluation. Various methods may be employed to determine the recreational sports needs and interests of a community including public hearings, focus groups, and citizen advisory councils. Mail or telephone surveys of the population are also typically conducted.

Goals and objectives both represent outcomes that an organization and participants seek to achieve. Goals are broad statements of purpose that help shape a agency's philosophy in terms of major outcomes to be achieved. Goals can be further broken down into objectives which specify short-term expectations. Objectives are specific, measurable program outcomes to be achieved within a set period of time.

There are two types of objectives that a program planner develops - *operational objectives* and *performance objectives*. Operational objectives are the methods used to conduct the program and typically include such factors as leadership, facilities and administration. Performance objectives are concerned with the program outcomes and describe the behavior or attitude that the program's participants should exhibit at its conclusion.

Selecting the "right" program alternative is generally based on its feasibility, practicality, and cost-effectiveness. Factors that must be considered when selecting a program include: Amount of human and financial resources required and available, dates, times, and program location.

The implementation stage involves a number of specific tasks, including: (1) designating personnel to leadership and supervisory positions, (2) developing a program promotional plan, (3) preparing a risk management plan to prevent accidents and maintain a safe recreation environment.

Activity evaluations are often the most neglected aspect of the recreation program planning process. Written evaluations and final program reports, if properly conducted, offer a wealth of information in planning an activity again and therefore should not be overlooked. Evaluation should be used to determine program response, eliminate safety hazards, and as a primary method of quality control.

This chapter has introduced the reader to the world of sport and outlined the basic steps involved in the sport program planning process. By adhering to these basic principles, the recreational sport planner may increase the effectiveness of her/his agency's programs and the opportunity for participant enjoyment.

## References

Bannon, J. J. (1976). *Leisure Resources: Its Comprehensive Planning*. Englewood Cliffs, New Jersey: Prentice-Hall.

Bartling, M. (1980). *Contracting Recreation and Park Services: Issues and Impacts*. Champaign, IL: Management Learning Laboratories.

Chambers, B. K. (1990). Quality is not dependent. *Parks and Recreation* 25(2): 6-7.

Corbin, D. & Williams, E. (1987). *Recreation: Programming and Leadership*. Englewood Cliffs, New Jersey: Prentice-Hall.

DeSensi, J., Kelley, D, Beitel, P. & Blanton, M. (1990). Sport management curricular evaluation and needs assessment: A multifaeted approach. *Journal of Sport Management*, 4(1): 31-58.

Eastman, S. & Meyer, T. Sports programming: scheduling, costs, and competition, In L. Wenner (Ed.), *Media, Sports and Scoiety*, Newbury Park, California: Sage Publications, Inc., 97-119.

Edginton, C. R., Crompton, D. M. & Hanson, C. J. (1980). *Recreation and Leisure Programming: A Guide for the Professional*. Philadelphia: W. B. Saunders.

Farre, P. & Lundegren, H. M. (1978). *The Process of Recreation Programming Theory and Technique*. New York: John Wiley.

Hoffman, F. W. & Bailey, W. G. (1991). *Sports and Recreation Fads*. Binghampton, New York: The Haworth Press, Inc.

Hoffman, D. & Greenberg, M. (1988). *Sport$biz*. Champaign, Illinios: Sagamore Publishing.

Howard, D. R. & Crompton, J. L. (1980). *Financing, Managing, and Marketing Recreation and Park Resources*. Dubuque, Iowa: Wm. C. Brown.

Kaiser, R. A. (1986). *Liability and Law in Recreation, Parks and Sports*. Champaign, Illinois: Sagamore Publishing, Inc.

Kraus, R. G. (1985). *Recreation Program Planning Today*. Glenview, Illinois: Scott, Foresman & Company.

Kraus, R. & Allen, L. (1984). *Research and Evaluation in Recreation, Parks and Leisure Studies.* Columbus, Ohio: Publishing Horizons.

Murphy, J. F., & Howard, D. R. (1977). *Delivery of Community Leisure Services: An Holistic Approach.* Philadelphia: Lea & Febiger.

Patterson, F. C. (1987). *A Systems Approach to Recreation Programming.* Worthington, Ohio: Publishing Horizons, Inc.

Reed, M. (1989). *IEG Legal Guide to Sponsorship.* Chicago: International Events Group, Inc.

Rossman, J. R. (1989). *Recreation Programming: Designing Leisure Experiences.* Champaign, Illinois: Sagamore Publishing.

Russell, R. V. (1982). *Planning Programs in Recreation.* St. Louis: C. V. Mosby.

Sandomir, R. (1988). The $50 billion sports industry, *Sports, Inc.*, November, 14, 14-23.

Sheffield, L. (1984). Are you providing multi-option programming? *Parks and Recreation*: May 56-57.

Theobald, W. F. (1979). *Evaluation of Recreation and Park Programs.* New York: John Wiley & Sons.

Tillman, A. (1973). *The Program Book for Recreation Professionals.* Palo Alto, California: National Press Book.

Turco, D. M. (1990). *A Market and Economic Analysis of the 1990 Red River Winter Carnival* (Technical report presented to the Town of Red River, New Mexico). Albuquerque, NM: University of New Mexico Bureau of Business and Economic Research.

Turco, D. M. & Bretting, J. G. (1990). Privatization in the public sector: Contracting out for leisure services. Presented at the AAHPERD Southwest District Annual Conference, February 8, 1990, Albuquerque, New Mexico.

# CHAPTER TWO
## Improving Sporting Events Through Market Planning

### Introduction
A market plan is a systematic analysis of an agency's resources, its competitors, its target markets, and the best promotional techniques to reach and influence those markets. The market plan embodies a sport agency's realistic intentions for competing successfully in the marketplace and should ultimately produce tangible results in terms of participants, sales, revenue and/or market share.

Private sector executives have long realized the importance of developing and implementing a market plan for successful management. The purpose of this chapter is to acquaint the recreational sports manager with basic marketing principles and to describe the major components of a marketing plan. In addition, this chapter is intended to serve as an "user-friendly" guide for sports programmers interested in developing a market plan for their agency. This may be accomplished by developing responses to the questions posed in each of the seven sections as applied to your sport operation or local environment.

### Market Planning
As illustrated in Figure 1, market planning is a continuous process involving the following activities: (1) service analysis; (2) competitor analysis; (3) determining target markets; (4) establishing goals and objectives; (5) developing action strategies; (6) implementation and (7) evaluation.

### Step One - Service Analysis
A sports program is a composite of want-satisfying characteristics. In designing a service, agencies should consider the "total service," which includes an assortment of auxiliary services as well as the primary offering. The total service of a municipal park and recreation department swimming program, for example, includes the facility, the timeliness of the program, the ease of registration, the type of participants assembled, and the courteous assistance of the instructor.

If a particular sport program or service does not receive the anticipated amount of participation or enthusiasm it is not necessarily because the targeted consumer group is disinterested. It may mean that the program or service is poorly promoted, provided in the wrong way or place, or offered at the wrong time or price.

A sport program or service and its distribution, price and promotion decisions comprise what is commonly termed the *marketing mix*. The following section contains a brief description of the four marketing mix components.

# MARKETING ACTIVITIES

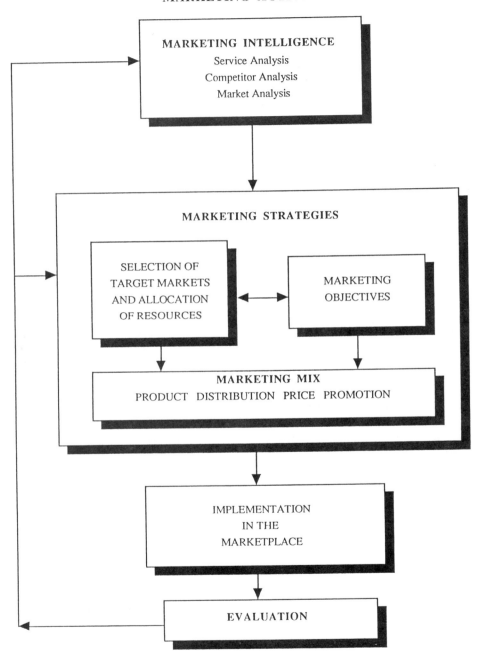

**MARKETING INTELLIGENCE**
Service Analysis
Competitor Analysis
Market Analysis

**MARKETING STRATEGIES**

SELECTION OF
TARGET MARKETS
AND ALLOCATION
OF RESOURCES

MARKETING
OBJECTIVES

**MARKETING MIX**
PRODUCT DISTRIBUTION PRICE PROMOTION

IMPLEMENTATION
IN THE
MARKETPLACE

**EVALUATION**

## The Marketing Mix
### Product or Service

Sport programs are comprised of numerous characteristics, each impacting the participant in various ways. A manager of a softball tournament must account for such program components as field conditions, officiating, registration, spectator comfort, and concessions - all of which comprise the softball tournament product or service. An effective marketing program requires that the attitudes and actions of each employee be client-orientated. Any employee, division, or department that is not client-orientated weakens the positive contribution of the entire agency. For example, if the person taking softball team walk-in program registrations is discourteous and abrupt, the potential client may assume that attitude is representative of the entire agency and seek to do business elsewhere.

Customers are concerned with the physical and psychological satisfaction they gain from using a service. Therefore, the sport marketer must approach the program or service from an image-conscious viewpoint. An important question that requires answering is, "How do users view our service? Prospects?" What is our department's reputation among its various consumers? The customers' perceptions will assist the agency in determining what service image to promote (positioning). Remember, emphasize and build upon service strengths while working to rectify service deficiencies.

### Distribution

Distribution is how services get to client groups where and when they want them.
1. How are facility locations selected?
2. Is the site visible and accessible to target markets?

Scheduling addresses the questions, "When is the best time to offer a service, for how long and for how often?" Clearly, if a service is not offered at the "right" time, client usage is less likely to occur. The primary rule for scheduling is that it should be governed by the needs of the targeted markets.

1. When are services made available to clients? (a) season of year; (b) day of week; (c) time of day? Are these times most appropriate?

2. How frequently are services offered? Are there multiple offerings? Are these decisions based on analysis of user preference or staff convenience? Past scheduling?

Forfeits occur occasionally in sports programs when a team or individual fails to show-up for a scheduled match. This behavior is disruptive and often financially costly to the organizing agency since fields may have been groomed and officials contracted for the match. Most sports organizers require participants to pay a forfeit fee at the beginning of the season which is then deducted for a forfeited match. The full fee is returned

23

to participants who complete the league or tournament without a forfeit. Participants who forfeit more than one game may be ineligible for the remainder of the competition and/or from participation in other agency-sponsored sports programs.

*Price*
       Price is what a user must give up in order to obtain the services offered. Many public sector park and recreation agencies that provide community sport programs are subsidized through the tax system, so service users do not pay the full price needed to cover the cost of a service. While price is usually expressed in dollar terms, money reflects only the direct cost of a service. Indirect costs such as waiting time and opportunity cost are also part of the total price.

1.  What method is used for establishing a service price in your agency? Is price based on covering service delivery cost, the competition's price or another strategy?
2.  What are the agency's objectives in pricing each game and seat?
       a. Do seat prices vary based on proximity to the playing field?
3.  What discounts to the basic fee structure are offered and with what rationale?
4.  What methods of payment are accepted (credit card, cash, check)?
5. Does your agency guarantee service delivery?

Price differentials are typically offered to the following population segments:

| | | |
|---|---|---|
| Age | Disabled | First-time participants |
| Residents/Nonresidents | Groups/Families | |
| Under 12 years | Timely users (Peak v. Off-peak Time) | |
| Over 55 years | | |

*Promotion*
       Promotion facilitates service purchase and/or usage by transmitting pertinent information about a service, its price and distribution to the targeted client groups. Promotion consists of four primary activities known as the *promotion mix*:  (1) personal selling; (2) publicity; (3) advertising; and (4) incentives.

1.  *Personal selling* is direct personal communication between recreation department representatives and prospective clients to encourage program or service usage.  Activities typically relying upon personal selling include recruiting and retaining customers and volunteers, fund-raising and lobbying.

2.  *Publicity* is a news or editorial message about a program or service transmitted through mass media at no charge to the recreation department.

# Member Benefits

## Free Fitness Orientation and Assessment

All members are entitled to a free fitness program orientation and assessment. This initial service will provide you with information about safe exercise, body fat measurements, flexibility and aerobic evaluation, introduce a complete exercise program, and advise you on safe use of equipment with optimal results.

*You can update your assessment for only $20 per hour, or ask the fitness floor staff any questions.*

## Free Equipment Orientation

Equipment orientations are offered at Courts Plus throughout the year at no cost.

## Personal Training

You can improive the quality and efficiency of workouts with our certified, experienced personal trainers. Learn to set and meet goals, achieve higher levels of fitness and push yourself with the guidance of personalized expert attention.

| | |
|---|---|
| One individual session | $22 |
| 3 individual sessions | $60 |
| 6 individual sessions | $110 |
| Group session fee | $30 for 6 weeks |

## Professional Massage Therapy

After those hard workouts – relieve stress! You can relax and relieve those aching muscles with a massage.

| | |
|---|---|
| Fee: | $20 - 30 minutes |
| | $35 - 60 minutes |

## Courts Plus Rentals

Courts Plus members may reserve court time for tennis, racquetball and/or wallyball parties on Saturdays from 7 p.m. to closing. Please confirm the number of courts, the time and commit with payment one week in advance of the reserved date.

## Staff Certifications

Courts Plus offers you experienced and certified staff to make your workouts safe and effective.

- All aerobic instructors are certified by the American Council on Exercise (A.C.E.).
- Fitness staff members have a bachelor's degree in physical education, undergraduate/graduate degrees in health and exercise physiology and some have master's degrees.
- All fitness instructors are in-house certified on exercise safety and correct equipment use.
- All staff members have CPR certificates.
- Aquatic Instructors are certified by Aquatic Exercise Association.
- Lifeguards are Ellis certified.

## New!
## Bearfoot Fun & Fitness Center

As an added benefit for Fitness Plus Family Memberships, each family will receive a free unlimited use punchcard for children ages 6 months to 5 years to attend open gym sessions at the new Bearfoot Fun and Fitness Center at Eldridge Park, located at 363 Commonwealth Lane. The new center offers children the opportunity to have fun and achieve fitness utilizing climbing and gym apparatus under the supervision of a qualified instructor. The punchcard is not applicable for the Bearfoot Fun and Fitness Center classes.

**An Elmhurst Park District Facility
186 S. West Ave., Elmhurst, Illinois**

Many public sector park and recreation departments receive publicity when league standings, league or race results are printed in the home town newspaper's sports section.

3. *Advertising* differs from publicity in that it must be paid for and the sponsor of the message is identified.

4. *Incentives* may be defined as direct inducements that offer extra value to encourage participation in a program or use of a service (Crompton & Lamb: 473). Incentives such as free trial offers, promotional prices, celebrity appearances and prizes are used by recreation departments in attempt to stimulate trial or increase usage by the targeted group. Some recreation department arts and craft classes, for example, allow interested persons to attend the first class free of charge and/or 2-for-1 registration fees.

For a promotional message to be effective, three conditions must occur: (1) it must gain attention; (2) address the needs and interests of the targeted user group; and (3) positively portray service image. Have your agency's previous promotional efforts accomplished these goals?

What media are currently being used by your agency to promote its sport programs? Table 1 provides a listing of media forms typically employed by recreational sport agencies to promote their services:

Table 1

| Forms of Mass Media | | |
|---|---|---|
| Television | Specialty Advertising | |
| Radio | Phone Lines | Word-of-mouth |
| Direct Mail | Transit | Newspapers |
| Brochures and Fliers | Magazines | Telephone Directories |
| Outdoor Advertising | Catalogs | |

## Key Questions for Sport Marketing

It is important to emphasize that promotion is only one of four components of the marketing mix. An effective promotional effort will not overcome poor service, pricing or distribution decisions.

1. Can program registration or inquiries be tracked to a particular form of advertising, publicity or personal selling? Are they seasonal? Have any of these factors changed in recent years?

2. Review past advertising and promotional campaigns. What was the strategy? Did it work? What was the rate of return on investment?

## Step Two - Competitor Analysis

It is important to conduct a comprehensive analysis of your competitors and position your services in such a way that stress your advantages over the competition. Competitors are agencies whose services compete for the same customer either directly by offering similar services, or indirectly by satisfying similar basic needs. Competitors to a municipal park and recreation department sports program may be a private fitness center, country club, resort, or other public agencies (i.e., school system, county park and recreation department). Describe and assess their marketing strategies by answering the questions below. Your competitor's service weaknesses may be your agency's strengths - stress your advantages over the competition in promotional messages.

1. Who is currently selling to your department's prospective customers?
2. What are the strengths and weaknesses of their service, their promotional techniques, their management?
3. What are their service images?

## Step Three - Determining Target Markets

An important task in planning and implementing marketing efforts is to identify potential target markets. Crompton and Lamb (1986: 128) define a target market as a relatively homogeneous group of people with relatively similar service preferences with which the agency seeks to do business. They describe the importance of this stage in the market planning process:

The identification and selection of target market groups influences and often directly determines all of the ensuing decisions that must be made regarding types of services, their distribution, pricing, and communication. Once target markets have been identified, everything the agency does must be tailored to the wants of the people in these groups.(p. 112)

The sports planner must first decide *whose* needs to serve before deciding *what* needs to serve. Markets for public park and recreation department offerings are comprised of people with wants and needs for particular programs and services possessing the ability and desire to purchase/use these programs and services. Who uses your agency's services?

## Market Segments

Markets are most often segmented by geographic, demographics and behavioral characteristics. Geographic descriptions are necessary but alone not sufficient for defining target markets. Boundaries for a neighborhood, city and/or county are commonly used as geographic segment descriptors. Zip codes are often used rather than physical boundaries in determining geographic market segments. Time travel and geographical distance can also serve as useful variables for identifying potential user groups.

Demographic variables are measurable characteristics of a group or segment such as age, gender, race, family size, education, occupation, and

27

income levels. Customers belonging to the same demographic group may have common needs and interests and will demand certain services.

People who share geographic and demographic characteristics *do not necessarily* consume leisure services in the same manner. Therefore, behavioral variables such as usage rate, stage of program consumption, skill level, and lifestyle are important in determining target markets. Clients may be segmented by the extent to which a particular service is used. User categories may include some combination of the following: nonusers, former users, potential users, first-time users, light or irregular users, medium users and heavy users.

Lifestyle or psychographic characteristics as a measure for target market segmentation measures people's activities in terms of how they spend their time, and their view of themselves and the world around them. Psychographic segmentation groups people according to their lifestyle or personality traits. For example, a Michigan tourism study classified "Sports Enthusiasts" as young (21-34 years), single males who participate in sports leagues year round. These individuals possess high ego and involvement levels relative to their athletic participation and are highly competitive. Their athletic equipment must be top-of-the-line. Sports Enthusiasts are motivated to compete by extrinsic factors (i.e., trophies and awards, etc.) as well as the comradeship associated with team play. When not participating, they attend or view televised sporting games and follow scores and standings in newspapers.

The major criteria for effective segmentation are that a segment should be (1) large enough to justify developing a specific marketing mix to service it, (2) of a measurable size, and (3) accessible to distribution and communication efforts. Ask and attempt to answer the following questions regarding the participants of a sport event:

1. Who are your current and probable future target markets?

2. Where are they from?

3. What do they like to do? What is known about the purchasing habits and attitudes of prospects? Include any information that more clearly describes your target populations so you have a better understanding of their wants, needs and desires.

4. How does a potential participant find out about your agency's sports services?

5. When do clients make their participation/purchase decisions? When do they decide to enroll in a sport workshop or class, enter a race or tournament? This information will assist you in knowing when to promote you service so it is in your customers' minds when they make their consumption decisions.

6. Why do they patronize you? Why don't they patronize you? Are your prices cheaper or more expensive than your competitors? Is your sport program superior? In what ways? Realizing your strengths and weaknesses will help you to promote your strengths and improve your weaknesses in addition to assisting you in determining the most effective message to reach these markets.

# THE X FACTOR: MARKETING SPORT TO GENERATION X

In 1995, individuals between 19 and 30 years totaled 44.6 million, representing 17 percent of the total United States population. This generation of young people has been labeled "twentysomethings" and the "13th generation," but these tags reveal nothing about the character of the generation. Worst of all the labels, "baby buster" suggests that this generation is a bust and not worth bothering about. Generation X as a label for young people born between 1965 and 1976 may be most appropriate since they are the most diverse and least like preceding generations.

The new generation of young adults is more interested in the visual arts, less active as sport spectators and more likely to live with their parents. Born into an increasingly diverse world, they are more likely than their elders to accept differences in race, ethnicity, national origin, sexual preferences, family structures, and lifestyles. Young adults like to exercise their eyeballs with art, TV, and movies, but are less fond of exercise for the rest of their bodies (Zill & Robinson, 1995). They have higher college attendance rates, but their graduation rates are unchanged and incomes are down. As managers of sport services, what impacts will the consumer behaviors of Generation X have on our operations?

Broad generalizations about any generation are likely to be inaccurate. But to bypass this generation because of its comparatively small size (baby boomers numbered 77.6 million in 1995; baby boomlets - those under 19 years, totaled 72.1 million) or to think that today's young adults are no different from others, would be a mistake. The purpose of this section is to describe Generation X and separate facts from misconceptions about them so that sport marketers can better reach and satisfy young adult consumers.


## SPORT & RECREATION

Compared with their counterparts of a decade ago, Xers are not as likely to engage in sports or outdoor recreation activities. The proportion of 18-24 year olds who engaged in such sports as softball, basketball, golf, bowling, tennis, or skiing in the last 12 months declined from 62 percent in 1982 to 59 percent in 1992. The proportion who went camping, hiking, or canoeing fell from 51% to 43% over the same period.

The share who reported jogging, lifting weights, walking, or engaging in other regular exercise did not change significantly, from 70 percent in 1982 to 67 percent in 1992. However, the overall proportion of adults who exercised increased during this time period from 51 percent to 60 percent. Further supporting the "couch potato" movement among some Xers, a study conducted by the National Center for Health Statistics revealed a 15 percent decline in fitness activities among young adults between 1985 and 1990; a decline twice as large as for older Americans.

When it comes to exercise, it appears that the slogan "Just say no." has more meaning to Xers than "Just do it."

Today's young adults are a shrinking proportion of professional and college sport spectators. In 1991, 18-24 year old comprised 13.6 percent of college football spectators; down 10.2 percent from 1984 (See Table 1). Young adults attending college basketball games declined 6.8 percent during the same period. Attendance at professional sports also declined from 1984 to 1991 for football (22.8% to 15.9%) baseball (20.2% to 14.2%) hockey (24.0% to 18.5%) and basketball (18.6% to 15.3%).

Table 1

### Sport Attendance Among Generation X, 1984-1991
#### Percentage of Total Spectator Base Age 18-24 years

| Sport | 1984 | 1987 | 1991 |
|---|---|---|---|
| Professional baseball | 20.2% | 16.7% | 14.2% |
| College basketball | 25.0 | 25.3 | 18.2 |
| Professional basketball | 18.6 | 24.7 | 15.3 |
| College football | 23.8 | 22.1 | 13.6 |
| Professional football | 22.8 | 19.3 | 15.9 |
| Ice Hockey | 24.0 | 23.9 | 18.5 |

Source: Simmons Market Research Bureau, Inc. 1984-1991

# ALTERNATIVES TO SPORT AMONG GENERATION X

Born into the television age, TV, movie, and vcr viewing are favorite pastimes among Xers. Eighteen-to-24 year olds report watching three hours of television on an average day. Are Xers watching sports on TV more often than previous generations? No. In 1991, they represented 12.3 percent of the television viewing audience for college football; down 4.4 percent from 1984 (See Table 2). Young adults watching college basketball games dropped 5.1 percent during the same period. Television viewing among young adults for professional sports also declined from 1984 to 1991 for football (17.9% to 13.9%) baseball (16.5% to 12.6%) and basketball (17.9% to 14.3%).

## Table 2

Sports Television Viewing Among Generation X, 1984-1991
Percentage of Total Sport Viewers Age 18-24 years

| Sport | 1984 | 1987 | 1991 |
|---|---|---|---|
| College basketball | 18.8% | 16.4% | 13.7% |
| Professional basketball | 17.9 | 17.0 | 14.3 |
| Professional baseball | 16.5 | 14.7 | 12.6 |
| College football | 16.7 | 15.6 | 12.3 |
| Professional football | 17.9 | 15.9 | 13.9 |

Source: Simmons Market Research Bureau, Inc. 1984-1991

Based upon a study conducted by the National Endowment for the Arts (1992), 82 percent of 18-24 year olds reported attending a movie in the last 12 months; considerably higher than the 59 percent movie attendance rate among adults of all ages. As revealed in Table 3, the proportion of young adults who attended films in 1992 surpassed the proportion who attended amusement parks (68%), amateur or professional sporting events (51%), historic parks or monuments (33%). Since 1982, attendance at amateur or professional sporting events dropped 14 percent among young adults, further supporting the previous evidence on their declining interest in attending traditional sports. Among those 18-24 years, 29% attended an art museum or gallery within the last 12 months compared with 23% in 1982. The percentage of young adults who would like to go to an art museum or gallery increased from 32% in 1982 to 42% in 1992. The percentage of 18-to-24 year olds who read any novels, short stories, plays or poetry in the previous 12 months fell from 60 percent in 1982 to 53 percent in 1992.

Table 3

Percent of Adults 18 to 24 Years who Attended Selected Places or Events in Previous 12 Months: 1982 and 1992

| Activity | 1982 | 1992 |
|---|---|---|
| Movies | 87% | 82% |
| Amusement or theme park | 67 | 68 |
| Amateur or professional sports event | 65 | 51 |
| Arts or crafts fair or festival | 35 | 37 |
| Historic park or monument | 34 | 33 |
| Stage play | 11 | 13 |

Source: U.S. National Endowment for the Arts, *Arts Participation in America: 1982 to 1992*.

## IMPORTANCE OF FAMILY

The divorce rate and the percentage of children born outside of marriage doubled between 1965 and 1977, the years in which today's young adults were born. More than 40 percent of today's young adults spent some time in a single-parent family by age 16. Because or in spite of these changing family patterns, today's young adults are perhaps closer to their parents than any recent generation has been. Nearly half of them continue to live at home through their late 20's and most Xers admire their parent(s) more than anyone else. Since young adults now remain at home longer, many marketers have underestimated their importance as consumers. Xers have become "designated decision makers" for their parents or relatives concerning recreational sport and electronic equipment. Direct promotional campaigns aimed at young adults should portray their dual roles as consumers and family decision makers.

Many Xers maintain contact with a vast network of relatives and friends, including several different family branches. To stay in touch and control with family contacts, e-mail, phones, beepers and pagers, answering machines, voice mail are necessities not luxuries to Generation X. Sport operations that provide ticket services and product purchase arrangements through personal computers will be favored by Xers.

Young people are reluctant to make personal sacrifices for the sake of the career. While Xer women will continue to work, they will not sacrifice their personal lives or families to the degree that baby boomer women did (Ritchie, 1995B). Xers are more likely to seek an equal balance of work and leisure activities than boomers were at their age. Sport, fitness, and recreation service providers that encourage family participation through tailored marketing mixes and embrace a broader definition of family beyond the traditional "Leave it to Beaver" model will be preferred by Generation Xers.

## SPORT MARKETING TO GENERATION X

Young adults have proved to be resistant to traditional marketing and advertising approaches, causing sport marketers to devise new marketing strategies to reach and influence them. Generation Xers are media critics and are highly sensitive to the authenticity of marketing messages (Schreiber, 1993). Xers don't dislike advertising. They dislike hype. They dislike over-statement, self-importance, hypocrisy, and the assumption that anyone would want to be disturbed by a salesperson on the telephone (Ritchie, 1995A). Sharp images, music, a sense of humor, and a dose of satire all appeal to a generation raised on MTV. Advertisements that admit they are ads are effective with Xers; a generation that has been saturated with media and advertising all their lives.

If you want Generation Xers to consumer your sport product or service, it should be perceived as a useful - not one to be purchased for reasons of status or to make a statement, but one that fulfills a genuine need (Ritchie, 1995B). Young people, particularly those without college educations, tend to reject the materialistic concept of conspicuous consumption. Witness the resurgence in popularity of the Converse canvass basketball shoes (a.k.a. Chuck Taylor's) among young adults.

Results from a 1993 survey of young adults conducted by Simmons Market Research Bureau suggest that Xers are less likely to look for brand names when shopping and more open to experimenting with new brands. Brand loyalty tended to increase with education among young adults; the most brand loyal were those with college degrees. Marketers of less well-known sporting goods who seek to introduce new products or penetrate new geographic markets may see higher product trial levels among young adult consumers.

Escalating ticket prices for traditional college and professional sports may, in part, explain the recent decline in attendance among 18-24 year olds. Value is important to Xers since their median weekly earnings between 1982 and 1992 fell 9 percent among men and 4 percent among women (Zill & Robinson, 1995). They are price sensitive and would take advantage of group or advanced ticket purchase discounts for sport services.

Unlike baby boomers, Xers do not tend to idolize their role models. The use and effectiveness of celebrities such as Andre Agassi or Dennis

Rodman has short-lived influence, if any to Xers. This pattern may make it difficult to successfully employ a celebrity spokesperson in advertising directed to this audience (Ritchie, 1995A). Instead of celebrity icons, they like to see the common person come out on top and they particularly respect the opinions of their own who get ahead.

Because many schools have in the last 5-10 years dropped mandatory elementary and secondary physical education requirements from their curricula and limited the provision of several varsity and intramural sports due to budgetary priorities and cutbacks, today's young adults do not possess the sport knowledge and skills to be educated sport consumers. Similarly, Hofacre and Burman (1992) suggest that increased numbers of dual-career and one-parent families may have influenced sport participation among children and ultimately, their consumer behavior as adults. Working parents in the 1970's may not have had the time, financial resources or knowledge to introduce or instruct their children in traditional sports. Consequently, many young adults have less experience and interest in these sports today as participants or spectators.

Outdoor volleyball, rock climbing, mountain biking, and in-line skating are the fastest growing participant sports among Generation X. Participation into these fast-paced and high-risk sports requires considerable initial investment, particularly when purchasing high-end equipment. However, once core products are purchased, recreational participation can be enjoyed at little or no cost.

Young people value cultural diversity. They have witnessed change in the composition of the U.S. population in cities such as Los Angeles, Miami, El Paso and San Antonio, where the aggregate total of blacks, Hispanics, Asians, and others exceeds fifty percent of the total population. They will not hesitate to support professional sport teams comprised of African Americans, Hispanics, and Asians. The racial or ethnic diversity of a team may actually be an attractive feature to Xers and should be highlighted in a team's promotional messages.

The quality of the core sport product is important to Generation Xers but so are the sport peripherals. Focus group interviews comprised of students 18-24 years of age at one NCAA Division I university revealed that going to a college game is the first of the evening's many social engagements. Pre-games tailgate parties, entertainment during intermissions, promotional contests, and post-game festivities may be of more interest to Generation Xers than the game itself and should be staged to attract more of them as spectators.

## Needs Assessment

Marketing involves delivering programs and services that people want and that they will consistently support, as opposed to delivering services or programs that the agency believes appropriate. An effective marketing plan accepts the notion of the consumer as the center of the agency's operations. It requires focusing on the wants of present and potential consumers of leisure services whenever decisions regarding an agency's services, their prices, location, scheduling and promotion are being considered. The needs assessment process generally reveals a wide range of service benefits potential users want. Since resources are limited and the agency will not be able to meet everyone's wants, priorities have to be established. The agency has to identify exactly which wants, and which sections of the community possessing those wants, it is going to serve. This process is termed the selection of client groups, or targeting. It is a critical decision because it guides all of the subsequent decisions the agency must make.

## Target Market Research

Thus far, numerous questions have been presented with little mention of how to generate the necessary information with which to respond. Some cost-effective methods to answer the previous target market questions include:

| | |
|---|---|
| 1. Personal interviews | 5. Local chamber of commerce data |
| 2. Mail or telephone surveys | 6. Trend analysis |
| 3. Program participant registration forms | 7. Participant evaluations |
| 4. Conversion studies | 8. Promotion tracking |
| (Ratio of inquiries to participants) | 9. Sport associations |

Questionnaires used in a market research survey conducted by the University of New Mexico for the Albuquerque International Balloon Fiesta are located in Appendix A. As with all surveys, researchers should be concerned with valid instrumentation, adequate sample size, random selection of respondents, and project cost. Primary market data collection can be an expensive and time-consuming project. As a result, many sport providers opt to use secondary market data resources to make promotional planning decisions. Sources of market research data include the National Sporting Goods Association, Sport Market Place Annual, and U.S. Census data.

The size, geographic distribution, existing level of awareness and socio-economic characteristics of the department's target market will influence the selection of the promotional mix components. If the size of the target market is small and concentrated in a relatively small geographic area, personal contact may be the most effective means for reaching these persons. Promotion and advertising may be the most effective promotional mixture to reach and influence larger markets dispersed over a large geographic area. Socio-economic characteristics such as age, education and income influence promotional mix decisions in several ways. For example, less educated people are difficult to reach through printed materials because they do not tend to read extensively. Similarly, lower-income customers may be more influenced by incentives than higher-income groups and adult populations are more likely to read newspapers than are youths.

Determining the target markets to which a service should be offered is a two-stage process. The first stage is concerned with identifying all of the heterogeneous groups in a market, each of which may be a potential target market. The second stage is to select which of these potential client groups the agency intends to serve with a particular service. Any of three strategies may be adopted for selecting target markets: (1) total market, (2) differentiated, and (3) concentrated.

Major sporting events such as an annual town softball championship generally have community-wide appeal, requiring a single marketing mix to effectively service everyone. Unfortunately, this approach, termed total market selection, is often used without considering the advantages of target marketing. Failure to properly analyze the needs of the total market may result in bland services with little appeal to prospects.

An agency which develops and utilizes a range of marketing mixes, each tailored to a particular target market enables the agency to adapt to the specific needs of each selected user group. For example, a park and recreation department fitness program may provide a range of classes for users with various fitness levels such as, Getting Started, Low Impact, Water-Aerobics, and Super Fit. This strategy is likely to involve higher costs since offering a program for various ability levels may require specialized instructors and/or equipment. The agency may choose this approach if total customer satisfaction and/or revenues produced exceed the extra cost of employing more skilled personnel or purchasing specialized equipment.

If an agency lacks the resources to service segments with a differentiated strategy, a concentrated approach may be pursued. Efforts are focused on only one or two client groups which are deemed the most appropriate or responsive. For example, a rap concert is likely to meet the needs of only one segment of the total market. An attempt to promote to all citizens would probably be less successful than selecting one segment and seeking to reach and influence this group.

## Step Four - Determine Objectives

After thoroughly analyzing the service or program and determining the needs and interests of targeted markets, marketing objectives should be developed. Marketing activities should be aimed at achieving results which will benefit the agency and its clients. Because objectives will be used in evaluating the success of the program or service, it is vital that they be measurable. Sound objectives clearly state what is desired, by how much and within a certain time period. Below are four examples of marketing objectives:

1. To achieve a High participant satisfaction level among contestants in the 1991 Midwest Regional Senior Olympics.

2. To increase 1991 summer softball tournament registration by 15 percent over last year's total.

3. To enroll 40 percent of 1990 fall beginner fitness class participants in 1991 winter fitness classes.

4. To increase 1991 playground program participation among children from city's southwest district by 10 percent over last year's total.

## Step Five - Action Strategies

Action strategies describe the specific activities that are to be taken to achieve market planning objectives and who will carry them out. Guidelines should be developed providing a written description of each target market and program, the needs of each target market to be met by each program, the selected marketing mix, and service standards (See Figure 2).

Figure 2

---

## Action Strategies

**Target Markets**

Define the target market geographically, demographically, and in attitudinal and behavioral terms.

**Programs**

Describe each program to be offered during the planning period and justify

its existence.

**Needs**

State the needs of each target market to be fulfilled by each program.

**Objectives**

Specify performance objectives for each target market and operational objectives

for each program.

**Price**

State overall pricing policy (i.e., free, subsidized, going rate, etc.), and discuss cost-benefit ratio.

**Distribution**

Specify program location and scheduling in relation to targeted markets.

**Promotion**

Describe and justify the promotional strategies for each target market and each program.

**Service**

What service standards are established? How are they monitored?

Based on "Action Program Guidelines" in J. L. Crompton & C. W. Lamb, *Marketing Government and Social Services*. New York: John Wiley & Sons, 1986, p.66.

---

At the completion of this stage, a checklist of marketing activities should be developed clearly responding to the following general questions:

1. What is to be done?
2. Where is it to be done?
3. When will it be completed?
4. Who is responsible for completing the task?

In designating who is responsible for implementing the market plan, it is important to involve key decision makers within the department. People who are involved in the market planning process from its inception are more likely to enthusiastically carry it out. If operating managers are not supportive of the plan, they may only give it lip service and impede its effectiveness. A planning approach emphasizing democratic involvement will lead to acceptance and commitment.

## Step Six - Implementation

It is understood that most managers can't really afford to do the best they know how; they just do the best they can. Preoccupied with responding to requirements that may already be too demanding, they should use common sense and adapt portions of the market plan to their own situation. This incremental approach to implementing the plan will reduce the likelihood of mistakes and inefficiencies from occurring as managers struggle to develop, implement and evaluate a full-scale market plan. Initially, seek to accomplish immediate and urgent marketing objectives. Once positive results are attained, you will have more confidence in conducting a comprehensive market plan.

## Step Seven - Evaluation

The last step in the market planning process is to assess your department's marketing efforts after the plan has been implemented. Attaining pre-determined objectives is the primary focus of the marketing effort. Therefore, evaluation, which identifies where and why the plan is or is not working, is most important. The true measure of the effectiveness of your program or service is whether or not customers are better off, worse off or unchanged as a result. If unsatisfactory results are born from the evaluation, it is necessary to further examine the situation. Set-backs may be attributed to changes in the marketplace, inaccurate needs and interests assessments, or limitations in the selected promotional mix. When causes of the problems are identified, proper steps can be taken to remedy the situation. Below are several questions which may provide a general framework to evaluate programs or services:

1. Is the program or service achieving its objectives?
2. Are the original program objectives still valid, necessary, relevant, and appropriate after the implementation stage?
3. Is the program or service influencing the target market it seeks to influence?
4. Has your agency selected the type of media that will best reach the designated client group?
5. Can the results of the program be explained by some other factor that does not include the program?
6. Is the program or service providing the resources or services that were originally intended?
7. Is the program producing outcomes that were not intended?
8. What are the actual costs of providing services to clients?
9. What spill-over effects does the program have on other government units, the private sector, and citizens?

Evaluation is a vital management tool. It not only measures the results of market planning efforts but also supports management decisions by providing a sound rationale for future action. Three approaches are typically used to measure the effectiveness of the market plan: (1) unsolicited customer feedback; (2) observation; and (3) survey measures. Once information is collected and analyzed, consider and decide upon various alternatives. The sport marketer must then determine what problems seem to be impeding growth or financial success and how these problems may be turned around into realistic opportunities.

## Integrated Sport Marketing

The future of sport marketing will see more use of integrated marketing campaigns. Integrated marketing refers to a comprehensive and coordinated effort to market services involving a range of strategies. Such marketing strategies may include product extensions, celebrity spokespersons, multi-media promotions, and sponsorship. Nike's recent promotional campaign provides an excellent example of integrated marketing.

Nike's Integrated Marketing Effort

| Core Product | Slogan | Logo | Product Extensions |
|---|---|---|---|
| Athletic shoes | Just do it. | Swoosh | Clothing Accessories |

| Promotions | Celebrities | Distribution | Events |
|---|---|---|---|
| TV ads | Andre Agassi | Nike Town | Race sponsors |
| Official team shoe | Michael Jordan | Factory outlets | Tournament sponsors |
| Billboards | Pete Sampras | Retail stores | |

## SUMMARY

A market plan is a systematic analysis of an agency's resources, its competitors, its target markets, and the best promotional techniques to reach and influence those markets. The market plan embodies a sport agency's realistic intentions for competing successfully in the marketplace and should ultimately produce tangible results in terms of participants, sales, revenue and/or market share. Market planning is a continuous process involving the following activities: (1) service analysis; (2) competitor analysis; (3) determining target markets; (4) establishing goals and objectives; (5) developing action strategies; (6) implementation and (7) evaluation.

A sport program or service and its distribution, price and promotion decisions comprise what is commonly termed the *marketing mix*. Distribution is how services get to client groups where and when they want them. Scheduling addresses the questions, "When is the best time to offer a service, for how long and for how often?" Price is what a user must give up in order to obtain the services offered and includes the direct and indirect costs of a service. Indirect costs such as waiting time and opportunity cost are also part of the total price. Promotion facilitates service purchase and/or usage by transmitting pertinent information about a service, its price and distribution to the targeted client groups. Promotion consists of four primary activities known as the *promotion mix*: (1) personal selling; (2) publicity; (3) advertising; and (4) incentives.

It is important to conduct a comprehensive analysis of your competitors and position your services in such a way that stress your advantages over the competition. Competitors are agencies whose services compete for the same customer either directly by offering similar services, or indirectly by satisfying similar basic needs.

A target market is a relatively homogeneous group of people with relatively similar service preferences with which the agency seeks to do business and are typically segmented by geographic, demographics and behavioral characteristics. Determining the target markets to which a service should be offered is a two-stage process. The first stage is concerned with identifying all of the heterogeneous groups in a market, each of which may be a potential target market. The second stage is to select which of these potential client groups the agency intends to serve with a particular service through market research. Various forms of market research exist including personal interviews, local chamber of commerce data, mail or telephone surveys, trend analysis, program participant registration forms, and conversion studies.

Marketing activities should be aimed at achieving results which will benefit the agency and its clients. Because objectives will be used in evaluating the success of the program or service, it is vital that they be measurable. Sound objectives clearly state what is desired, by how much and within a certain time period.

In writing an action plan, guidelines should be developed providing a written description of each target market and program, the needs of each target market to be met by each program, the selected marketing mix, and service standards. At the completion of this stage, a checklist of marketing activities should be developed clearly stating who is responsible for what task and designated completion dates.

An evaluation of the sport marketing plan is important since it identifies where and why the plan is or is not working. Three approaches are typically used to measure the effectiveness of the market plan: (1) unsolicited customer feedback; (2) observation; and (3) survey measures.

## READINGS

The following publications are recommended for those seeking additional information on market planning:

Bangs, D. H. (1987). *The Market Planning Guide*. Montpilier, NH: Upstart Publishing Company, Inc.

Barndt, C. A. & Dry, E. (1989). *How to Design an Effective Tourism Marketing Plan: A Handbook for Small Businesses and Communities*. Albuquerque: University of New Mexico.

Crompton, J. L. & Lamb, C. W. (1986). *Marketing Governmental and Social Services*. New York: John Wiley & Sons.

Crompton, J. L. (1987). *Doing More With Less in Parks and Recreation Services*. State College, PA: Venture Publishing, Inc.

Crompton, J. L. Recreation vouchers: A case study in administrative innovation and citizen participation, *Public Administration Review 43*, 6, (November/December 1983) 537-546.

Crossley, J. C. (1986). *Public/Commercial Cooperation in Parks and Recreation*. Columbus, Ohio: Publishing Horizons, Inc.

Davidson, J. P. (1988). *Marketing on a Shoestring*. New York: John Wiley & Sons.

Deran, E. (1987). *Low-Cost Marketing Strategies*. New York: Praeger.

Dodge, W. R. Gift catalogues: The marketing technique for new revenue sources, *Parks and Recreation* (August 1982): 22.

Hofacre, S. & Burman, T. (1992). Demographic changes in the U.S. into the 21st Century: Their impact on sport marketing. *Sport Marketing Quarterly, 1*(1):31-36.

Kotler, P. (1982). *Marketing for Nonprofit Organizations* (2nd ed.) Englewood Cliffs, NJ: Prentice-Hall.

Kraus, R. G. & Curtis, J. E. (1986). *Creative Management in Recreation, Parks and Leisure Services*. St. Louis: Mosby College Publishing.

Lovelock, C. H. & Weinberg, C. B. (1989). *Marketing for Public and Nonprofit Managers*. Redwood City, CA: Scientific Press.

Makens, J. C. (1985). *The Marketing Plan Workbook*. New Jersey: Prentice-Hall, Inc.

Mitchell, S. How to talk to young adults. *American Demographics, 15*(4): 50-54.

NEA. (1993). The 1992 Survey of Public Participation in the Arts. Washington, DC: U.S. National Endowment for the Arts.

Reed, M. H. (1990). *The IEG Legal Guide to Sponsorship*. Chicago: International Events Group.

Riley, R. T. (1988). *Travel and Tourism Marketing Techniques*. Albany, NY: Delmar Publishers, Inc.

Ritchie, K. (1995A). *Marketing to Generation X*. American Demographics, 17(4): 24-33.

Ritchie, K. (1995B). *Marketing to Generation X*. New York: Lexington Books, Inc.

Stephenson, H. & Otterson, D. (1986). *Marketing Your Products and Services Successfully*. Los Angeles: Oasis Press.

Schreiber, A. (1993). Generation X the next big event target. *Advertising Age, 64*(26): S3.

Simmons Market Research Bureau, Inc. (1993). *Simmons Media and Market Survey - 1984 to 1993*. New York: SMRB, Inc.

Turco, D. M. (1991). *Economic Impact and Market Assessment of the 1991 Albuquerque International Balloon Fiesta*. Technical report prepared for the Albuquerque International Balloon Fiesta, Inc., Albuquerque, NM.

U.S. Census Bureau. (1994). *Population Projections of the United States, by Age, Sex, Race, and Hispanic Origin: 1992 to 2050* (Series P25-1104). Washington, D.C.: Government Printing Office.

Zill, N. & Robinson, J. (1995). The Generation X difference. *American Demographics, 17*(4): 24-33.

# CHAPTER THREE
## Consumer Satisfaction & Service Quality

### Understanding Marketing

Marketing is much more than selling or promoting a service or product. It requires directing an organization's human, financial and physical resources toward customers in order that they may be satisfied. Successful sport marketing requires that your organization meets or exceeds the expectations of the customer during every encounter or transaction. The sayings, "Never promise more than you can deliver, but always deliver more than you promised," and "Customer satisfaction is our first priority," are the mottos of an organization with a true marketing philosophy.

While it is important to understand the factors most influential to consumers in their decision to purchase a sport service, it is equally important to determine why some members of a target market do not. This section examines several constraints to sport participation and identifies strategies to minimize the impacts and encourage service consumption.

### Constraints

There are several reasons why people do not participate in sport. The leisure constraint literature yields the following:

*What factors constrain one's participation in leisure services?*
- Work commitments
- Overcrowded service site
- Difficulty finding others with whom to participate
- Location and access
- Lack of service knowledge
- Programmer-imposed restrictions
    o Age, gender, family structure

As sport programmers we often impose participation age restrictions without consideration of the physical or cognitive skills of the prospective consumer. Why? We assume, for example, that children under 12 years of age do not have the speed, strength and stamina, of those 13-15 years (even though some do) and therefore, bar them from competing against older youths. When appropriate, sport marketers should not group consumers by age but rather, assess the individual needs of the consumer and act on their behalf.

*Common reasons for not participating in sport services:*
- Site location
- Lack of interest in service
- Time
- Physical or cognitive ability
- Safety concerns

- Social stigma
- Financial cost
- Consume alternative services

*What can sport programmers do to remove obstacles to participation?*

**Barrier:    Financial  Cost**
   Offer down payment plans
   Utilize price fencing options
   Accept credit card payment

**Barrier:    Time**
   Offer multiple sections of services at varying times
   Provide on-site child care services

   Allow consumers to purchase services in small time intervals.  For example, instead of scheduling an 8-week summer tennis camp, break up the camp into four, two-week sessions to allow consumers who may be vacationing at some point to enroll without missing a significant portion of the program.

**Consumer  Decision-Making**
   The consumer decision-making process is cyclical in nature (See Figure 1).  Consumers first must recognize, either consciously or subconsciously, that a personal need to consume sport exists.  From this realization the consumer may actively seek information from the marketplace on how to satisfy this need.  Advertising, word of mouth referrals, and other promotions transmitted through communication channels also create awareness of sport service providers for the consumer.  Based on the information gathered and processed, the consumer evaluates her/his purchase options and a decision is reached to buy a sport service.  The service is subsequently consumed and evaluated.  Upon completion of the service, the consumer will either repeat consumption based on receipt of a satisfactory experience, seek alternative service providers because of marginal dissatisfaction, or drop-out due to extreme dissatisfaction.

1.  Why factors influence consumers' selection of services?
       Financial risk
                        **High risk**


| Routine | Extended |
|---|---|
| Decision Making | Decision Making |


                        Low risk

Sport Marketing Orientation

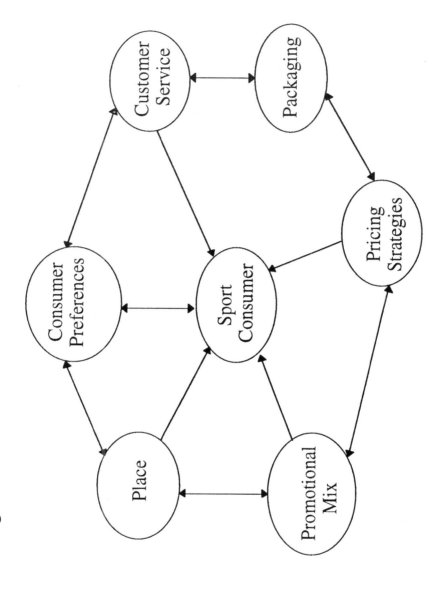

## Dimensions of Service Quality

Zeithal, Parasuraman, and Berry (1990) identified ten components of service quality. As managers of service organizations, we must strive to ensure that we and our staff achieve the highest levels of performance in each of these categories.

1. TANGIBLES: Appearance of physical facilities, equipment, personnel, and communication materials.

2. RELIABILITY: Ability to perform the promised service dependably and accurately.

3. RESPONSIVENESS: Willingness to help customers and provide prompt service.

4. COMPETENCE: Possession of required skills and knowledge to perform the service.

5. COURTESY: Politeness, respect, consideration, and friendliness of contact person.

6. CREDIBILITY: Trustworthiness, believability, honesty of the service provider.

7. SECURITY: Freedom from danger, risk, and doubt.

8. ACCESS: Approachability and ease of contact.

9. COMMUNICATION: Keeping customers informed in language they can understand and listening to them.

10. UNDERSTANDING THE CUSTOMER: Making an effort to know the customers and their needs.

From these ten service quality elements, five distinct dimensions were revealed. They are listed in order of importance to the customer:

1. **Reliability:** Ability to perform the promised service dependable and accurately.

2. **Assurance:** Knowledge and courtesy of employees and their ability to convey trust and confidence.

3. **Responsiveness:** Willingness to help customers and provide prompt service.

4. **Empathy:** Caring, individualized attention the agency provides its customers.

**5. Tangibles:** Appearance of physical facilities, equipment, personnel, and communication materials.

What customers are trying to tell us as providers of sport services is you must appear neat and organized, be responsive, be reassuring, be empathetic, and most of all, be reliable - do what you say you are going to do.

## Service Quality Gaps

There are several reasons why discrepancies exist between what consumers expect from sport services and what producers provide. As sport providers with a marketing orientation, we must constantly seek to satisfy our customers' needs and wants. This requires knowing what they want and do not want and assessing their perceptions of service quality. Zeithaml, Parasuraman, and Berry (1990), identified several gaps in the way customers and providers perceive service quality. In the final analysis, it is really the customer's perspective of service quality that matters.

## GAP #1: Not Knowing What Customers Expect

A lack of market research and customer service focus are the reasons Gap #1 exists in some sport organizations.

## GAP #2: The Wrong Service Quality Standards

The discrepancy between managers' perceptions of customers' expectations and the actual specifications they establish for service delivery.

## GAP #3: The Service Performance Gap

The difference between service specifications and the actual service delivery is the service-performance gap.

## GAP #4: When Promises do not Match Delivery

## Methods for Understanding Customers' Expectations

| Methods and Uses | Investments | |
|---|---|---|
| | Money | Time |
| **Strategic use of complaints**<br>Identifying problems in the service process | Low | Low |
| **Customers' desires in similar industries**<br>Developing an initial framework for customers; expectations in focal industry | Low | Low |
| **Research on intermediate customers**<br>Efficient way to gain in-depth information on selected customers | Moderate | Moderate |
| **Key client studies**<br>In-depth information on most important customers | Moderate | Moderate |
| **Customer panels**<br>Continuous source of information on changing customers; expectations | Moderate-high | Moderate-high |
| **Transaction-based studies**<br>Provides feedback on service quality performance of each component of service quality. | Moderate | Moderate |
| **Comprehensive customers' expectations studies**<br>Establishes measures that are customer-based; provides foundation for tracking studies which provide a dynamic view of customers; expectations and perceptions. | High | High |

Adapted from Zeithaml, V. A., Parasuraman, A., & Berry, L. L. (1990). *Delivering Service Quality*. New York: Macmillan Press, Inc.

# Sport Marketing Research

What would you like to know about your organization and the people it serves? To help your thought process, here are some questions sport marketers ponder on a regular basis:

Q: Who is consuming our services?

Q: Why are others not consuming our consumers?

Q: When do consumers decide to purchase our services or those of our competitors?

Q: What information is of most influence in consumers' decision-making process?

Q: Who are our direct competitors? What are our competitive advantages and short-comings?

Q: What is the economic impact of our operations on the local economy? How much tax revenue is generated by our operations?

Q: What is the demand for and revenue potential of additional or expanded services?

Q: How satisfied are participants/spectators with our services?

There must be a reason for asking the above questions. Here are some reasons why sport marketers want to know the answers to the previously posed questions:

+ Measure consumer satisfaction; Better serve visitors/consumers
+ Justify resource allocations
+ Identify and describe present/prospective markets - tailor marketing mix accordingly
+ Determine promotional effectiveness
+ Aid in securing/retaining sponsorship
+ Aid in securing advertising sales

There is one way to answer these questions - conduct market research. This section will explore the wide world of sport marketing research by providing numerous examples and issues associated with data collection and treatment.

# Sport Marketing Research

The most market research studies in sport involve profiling consumer markets, measuring the promotional effectiveness of the organization, estimating economic impact of sport operations, and gauging customer satisfaction.

## Market profiles

Market characteristics often profiled include
Geographic markets
Demographics
Attitudes, opinions and interests
Benefits sought from participation

## Promotional effectiveness research

*Conversion studies* - Examines the percentage of people who inquired about your services and ultimately purchased such services.

*Sponsor recall* - Spectators' ability to recall advertising signs at sporting events and the extent to which such signs influence their consumer decision making processes.

*Economic impact* - Measurement of the direct spending induced by an event within a designated economy.

*Customer satisfaction*

Importance-performance evaluations measure the importance of selected sport variables on customer satisfaction, and how well the sport organization is delivering these sport services.

### Research Considerations

Before conducting a sport marketing research project there are more questions that you must ask and answer. Given its time constraints and human and financial resources, can your organization effectively implement a market study or is outside assistance necessary? Below are other considerations before embarking on the path of market research:

## Time

Do the people in my organization have the time to take on one more large project?

## Know-how

Are there people in my organization with the skills and knowledge to successfully complete a valid research project? Who will analyze the data?

## Person Power

Does my organization have the human resources available to collect primary market data?

## Dollars and Sense: How much accuracy can we afford?

Can my organization afford the financial cost to plan and implement a study requiring primary data collection? Can we afford not to do the study?

## Who you gonna call?

If the study cannot be done internally, who can conduct the study for my organization?

## Research: Primary or Secondary?

Market research data comes in two forms: Primary and secondary. Primary data are collected directly from the participant or consumer. Focus groups and customer surveys conducted by your organization are examples of primary data data sources. Secondary data are collected and analyzed by another source. The data are not second-hand, only maintained by an outside party. U.S. Bureau of the Census data and statistics from the National Sporting Goods Association or Simmons Market Research are examples of secondary data sources.

## Survey Biases

There are several contaminants to the validity and reliability of market research. These biases are briefly described below:

## Nonresponse Bias

Contaminates survey reliability and eats away at generalizability.

## Selection Bias

Rather than systematically selecting a sample, visitors for interviews are sampled based on their pleasant appearance.

## Location Bias

Sampling only residents in a relatively homogeneous sector of a community may distort the view of the total population.

## Recall Bias

Acute in economic impact studies involving the mail-back survey technique with a lengthy time lag.

## SAMPLING

A common question in event market research involving primary data collection is, "How many people must I survey?" Unless the entire population of spectators, participants, or residents is surveyed, the results of your research will have some degree of variability or error. Populations over 100,000 are considered infinitely large require systematic sampling. A sample size of 400 persons will produce results accurate to within ± 5% of the actual reported figure at a 95% confidence interval; a sample of 625 yields results ± 4%; 1,111 generates a ± 3% range.

Since greater sample sizes often lead to added time and money, the administrator must decide how much variability she or he is willing to accept in the study. Samples sizes in economic impact studies should be large enough for a ± 4% to ± 5% tolerated error level.

| Population | | Precision Levels | | |
|---|---|---|---|---|
| Size | ±3% | ±4% | ±5% | ±10% |
| 10,000 | 1,000 | 588 | 385 | 99 |
| 20,000 | 1,053 | 606 | 392 | 100 |
| 50,000 | 1,087 | 617 | 397 | 100 |
| 100,000 | 1,099 | 621 | 398 | 100 |
| Over 100,000 | 1,111 | 625 | 400 | 100 |

Source: Yamane, T. (1967). Elementary Sampling Theory. Englewood Cliffs, NJ: Prentice-Hall.

## Survey Location

Where to collect primary event information from spectators is often as difficult a question to answer as how it should be collected. Interviews conducted at exits tend to experience higher nonresponse rates than entrance or on-site interviews, especially at crowded evening events. Most patrons exiting are interested in getting to their cars and beating the traffic out of the parking lot - not stopping to answer a few questions.

## Survey Scheduling

It is not practical nor recommended to sample participants or event spectators during every hour of operation. Selection of days and hours of operation to sample event spectators should be done at random to control for sampling bias and assure generalizability of results to the total population of spectators.

For multi-day events with at least eight hours of operation per day, a recommended survey schedule is to establish two hour time periods to conduct the survey. These time periods should be randomly selected from all possible hours of the event. An example of the survey schedule used for the economic impact study of the Men's Fast Pitch Softball National Championship Tournament held in Bloomington, Illinois is found below.

Survey Schedule
ASA Men's Fast Pitch Softball National Championship Tournament, Bloomington, Illinois

| Day | Time | Sample Size |
|---|---|---|
| Friday, Sept. 11 | 6:30-9:30 p.m. | 60 |
| Saturday, Sept. 12 | 12:30-3:00 p.m. | 60 |
| | 6:00-8:30 p.m. | 60 |
| Sunday, Sept. 13 | 12:30-3:00 p.m. | 60 |
| Monday, Sept. 14 | 12:30-3:00 p.m. | 50 |
| Thursday, Sept. 17 | 6:00-8:30 p.m. | 50 |
| Friday, Sept. 18 | 6:30-9:00 p.m. | 50 |
| Total | | 390 |

Another survey scheduling technique is to stratify survey implementation based upon anticipated or past event attendance. At the Kodak Albuquerque International Balloon Fiesta, approximately 20 percent of the total event attendance occurs during the first day; therefore, approximately 20 percent of the total number of surveys are administered during the first day.

## Contracting out Research Services

If your organization does not have the ability to conduct survey research, consider enlisting the services of an outside firm. Below are some considerations when seeking the research services of an external firm:

Adhere to agency's standardized contract bid procedures
Specify time-lines and deliverables in RFP
Require selected firms to present their bid formally to the board
Check each firm's previous clients and references
Review and approve all methods/questions before implementation
Require progress reports from contracted firm
Build in follow-up analysis into RFP
Retain the data and results on diskette

# SOLVING PROBLEMS THROUGH MARKET RESEARCH

## TEAM APPROACH TO SOLVING PROBLEMS USING MARKET RESEARCH

**TASK:** Each team is responsible for developing a data collection strategy that will enable you to solve your specific leisure services problem. Your specific charges are listed below. Good Luck!

+    Devise a research approach and plan for action. Will you conduct a phone, mail, or in-person survey? When will you collect the data? What is the best way to collect data in order to solve your team's administrative problem? Please justify your team's decisions.

+    **Design a sampling frame.** Whom do you plan to collect data from and why? Is your sample a representative of the population?

+    **Formulate questions for a survey instrument.** What sorts of questions will you ask your respondents? Design an adequate number of questions that will allow you to start solving your management problem.

+    **Discuss how you will use the data collected to assist your team in problem solving.** How do you intend to influence decision making with the results of your study? How will you present the findings? Which format will you use: Report, board meetings, staff meetings, press conference, annual report, other forms of media?

# MARKET RESEARCH CASE STUDIES

## SHOOT-THE-BIRD

The 5th Annual Shoot-the-Bird 3-on-3 basketball tournament will be held June 14-16, 1996 in Bloomington, Illinois. Participants compete in gender and wheelchair divisions based upon the skills and basketball experience level of their team. This event is financed, in part, by the Town of Normal ($3,000 contribution), City of Bloomington ($4,000), and the Bloomington-Normal Area Chamber of Commerce ($1,000) and is intended to benefit the Illinois Special Olympics. The previous four Shoot-the-Birds have been plagued by poor weather and planning. Shoot-the-Bird has made only $6,300 for the Special Olympics in four years. Violence erupted at the event last year as some opponents began fighting; police had to be summoned to stop fisticuffs on two separate occasions.

The event will be held in the parking lots between Redbird Arena and Horton Fieldhouse on the campus of Illinois State University - the third location for the event in its brief history (the other event sites were downtown streets in Normal and indoors in Horton Fieldhouse). The past two years, participation in Shoot-the-Bird has averaged 2,000 players. Other 3-on-3 tournaments in central Illinois have drawn as many as 10,000 participants.

No research has ever been done on this event. The mayors of Normal and Bloomington have requested a study be conducted to participant satisfaction with Shoot-the-Bird. "I will not give Shoot-the-Bird another dime until I am convinced it is a benefit to the community," exclaimed Bloomington Mayor, Jesse Smart during a recently televised city council meeting. Cost over runs have again hit Shoot-the-Bird; no money will be available to conduct the study other than for printing. As a member of the Shoot-the-Bird planning team comprised of sport managers from Normal and Bloomington, how will you measure participant satisfaction? What questions will you ask consumers to determine their satisfaction? How will you measure the value of the event?

## PLAY BALL IN BLOOMINGTON?

Owners of the Class A minor league baseball franchise, Omaha Cornhuskers (a Cleveland Indian affiliate) are considering a deal to relocate their team to Bloomington-Normal, Illinois. The Cornhuskers have averaged 3,100 spectators per home game over the last four seasons but the team has not turned a profit since 1988. Several team alums have gone on to play in the big leagues including Chipper Jones, Jim Thome, and Jose Offerman.

Members of the McLean County Chamber of Commerce and the McLean County Executive Development Council have endorsed the idea of "bringing baseball to the America's heartland." Team officials request that before a commitment to bring the team to the Twin Cities is made, a state-of-the-art minor league stadium must be developed. The stadium will be multiple-use in design and be financed entirely by taxpayers.

A consortium of franchise owners, local politicians, and investors have asked you to determine the spectator interest and demand for minor league baseball in the Bloomington-Normal area and its economic impacts. How will you do this? Describe in detail the methods you would use to determine the demand and economic impact of this operation. Include data sources, collection strategies, and questions you would pose to prospective consumers in order to respond to the local officials' request.

## Market Research Assignment

Select one of the following sport/recreation services:

| | |
|---|---|
| Aerobic dance participants | Golfers in your hometown |
| In-line skaters: Recreational and competitive | High school sport spectators |
| Local running racers | University men's football spectators |
| Local 3-on-3 basketball competitors | Local anglers |
| Local sand volleyball competitors | Softball league participants |
| Local indoor soccer participants | Local cyclists |
| Proposed indoor ice rink | Other (specify)_____ |

Using secondary and/or primary market research available on the chosen sport/recreation service, complete the following four tasks:

(1) Identify consumer service needs and preferences as well as existing service suppliers;

(2) describe consumer demand trends (since 1980) and demand projections (to 2000);

(3) provide a consumer profile in terms of demographic, geographic, and psychographic variables; and,

(4) offer recommendations to suppliers so that they may reach and deliver quality services to consumers.

CONSIDER: Sport governing bodies and professional associations, trade publications, National Sporting Goods Association, Simmons Market Research, U.S. Bureau of the Census, local recreation/sport organizations.

## Discussion Questions

1. Discuss the three fundamental ways services differ from goods by offering examples of the differences within a sport/recreation context. Why is service quality more difficult to evaluate than goods quality?

2. What are the various dimensions of service quality? Identify each within and/or void from a sport/recreation enterprise.

3. Identify the benefits of reliable service to a sport organization.

4. What are the challenges to delivering reliable sport/recreation services? What activities can an organization take on to avoid these failures? Provide examples of these activities within the context of a sport/recreation service delivery system.

## References

Berry, L. L. & Parasuraman, A. (1991). Doing the service right the first time. *Marketing Services.* New York: The Free Press.

Zeithaml, V. A., Parasuraman, A. & Berry, L. L. (1990). The customers' view of service quality. *Delivering Service Quality.* New York: The Free Press.

# CHAPTER FOUR
## Round Robin Tournaments

Where time, resources, and facilities permit, the round robin tournament is recommended over all other types of tournaments since it allows every team or individual to play every other entry an equal number of times. A round robin tournament allows every entry to play every other entry regardless of record or ability. The winner is determined by the team or individual with the highest percentage of matches won. The round robin format is often used to develop league schedules. To play a round robin tournament, you must have an equal amount of team positions. If you have an odd number (i.e., n=7), you would add one BYE and increase the number to eight.

To set up and play a round robin tournament, you back number the teams entered. If there are an odd number of teams entered, add one BYE to even the number. The BYE will be placed in the last position. Once all teams are in place, keep team one in a fixed position and rotate all the other teams and BYE if needed one position to the left until arriving one position before the start. The number of rotations is one less than the number of the positions in the tournament.

Figure 1 contains an example of the rotation scheduling format applied to an eight team round robin tournament. The first round of the tournament features the following games: Braves v. Expos; Brewers v. Cardinals; Orioles v. Cubs; and Tigers v. Mariners. The second round features a new series of games: Braves v. Cardinals; Expos v. Cubs; Brewers v. Mariners; and Orioles v. Tigers. Notice that the position of Team One (Braves) remains fixed throughout the rotation process and that the other teams rotate in a counter-clockwise direction around Team One for each successive round of the tournament. Had only seven teams entered the tournament, the position occupied by Team 8 (Expos) would have been assigned a BYE (See Figure 2).

When the number of entries in a league is large, it may be more practical to divide them into leagues of 4 to 12 entries and run a separate round robin for each league than attempt to place them all in the same round robin.

League competition often has two phases. First, a round robin tournament in each league to determine the champion of each league; and second, an elimination tournament bringing together the league champions to determine the championship of the entire tournament.

## Figure 1

### ROUND ROBIN SCHEDULING

#### ROUND ONE
| | |
|---|---|
| 1 - Braves | 8 - Expos |
| 2 - Brewers | 7 - Cardinals |
| 3 - Orioles | 6 - Cubs |
| 4 - Tigers | 5 - Mariners |

#### ROUND TWO
| | |
|---|---|
| 1 - Braves | 7 - Cardinals |
| 8 - Expos | 6 - Cubs |
| 2 - Brewers | 5 - Mariners |
| 3 - Orioles | 4 - Tigers |

#### ROUND THREE
| | |
|---|---|
| 1 - Braves | 6 - Cubs |
| 7 - Cardinals | 5 - Mariners |
| 8 - Expos | 4 - Tigers |
| 2 - Brewers | 3 - Orioles |

#### ROUND FOUR
| | |
|---|---|
| 1 - Braves | 5 - Mariners |
| 6 - Cubs | 4 - Tigers |
| 7 - Cardinals | 3 - Orioles |
| 8 - Expos | 2 -Brewers |

#### ROUND FIVE
| | |
|---|---|
| 1 - Braves | 4 - Tigers |
| 5 - Mariners | 3 - Orioles |
| 6 - Cubs | 2 - Brewers |
| 7 - Cardinals | 8 - Expos |

#### ROUND SIX
| | |
|---|---|
| 1 - Braves | 3 - Orioles |
| 4 - Tigers | 2 - Brewers |
| 5 - Mariners | 8 - Expos |
| 6 - Cubs | 7 - Cardinals |

#### ROUND SEVEN
| | |
|---|---|
| 1 - Braves | 2 - Brewers |
| 3 - Orioles | 8 - Expos |
| 4 - Tigers | 7 - Cardinals |
| 5 - Mariners | 6 - Cubs |

## Figure 2

### Round Robin Schedule With BYE

| ONE | TWO | THREE | FOUR | FIVE |
|---|---|---|---|---|
| 1 - BYE | 1 - 7 | 1 - 6 | 1 - 5 | 1 - 4 |
| 2 - 7 | BYE - 6 | 7 - 5 | 6 - 4 | 5 - 3 |
| 3 - 6 | 2 - 5 | BYE - 4 | 7 - 3 | 6 - 2 |
| 4 - 5 | 3 - 4 | 2 - 3 | BYE - 2 | 7 - BYE |

| SIX | SEVEN |
|---|---|
| 1 - 3 | 1 - 2 |
| 4 - 2 | 3 - BYE |
| 5 - BYE | 4 - 7 |
| 6 - 7 | 5 - 6 |

To determine the number of games to be played for administration purposes, use the following formula. Remember, omit all BYE games. For the previous example, 28 games were scheduled.

$$G = [N \times (N-1)] \div 2$$
$$G = 8 \times 7 \div 2$$
$$G = 28$$

Where:     N = Number of teams entered in the round robin tournament
G = Number of games to be played in the round robin tournament

## Round Robin Practice Problem

The following teams have entered your round robin tournament: Rattlesnakes, Coyotes, Roadrunners, Hawks, Armadillos, Wolves, Lions, Bears, and Moles. Set up the tournament and rotate the teams. How many total games are scheduled for the tournament?

## Tie-Breakers

A potential drawback of round robin tournament is that after playing the full schedule, two or more teams may finish with identical win-loss records. In the event of a tie, one of the following tie-breaking methods should be used:

1. If time permits, schedule play-offs between or among the tied teams.

2. Allow ties to stand and name co- or tri-champions if the tie involves first place.

3. Head-to-head record - Two-way ties may be resolved by awarding a higher position to the team which beat the other tied team in their head-to-head match-up. For example, Team A would receive a higher position because it defeated the other tied team, Team B, during league play.

4. Two-way ties may be broken by accounting for the differences in teams' scores. Subtracting the difference between total offensive and defensive points provides a positive or negative factor. The team with the greatest positive factor is awarded first place.

## League Standings

Once the sports league is underway and teams have completed several games they will want to know where they stand in relation to the other competing teams. League standings are typically calculated to provide information on a team's win-loss records, winning percentage, ranking or place within the league, and the number of games behind the first-place team.

## Winning Percentage

Place or ranking of league participants is usually based on a team's winning percentage which is determined by dividing the total number of wins by the total number of games played (WP = W ÷ TG). Usually the winning percentage is calculated to three places to the right of the decimal point. For example, if the Green Bay Packers had a win-loss record of 10 wins and 6 losses, their winning percentage would be .625 (10 wins ÷ 16 total games). League participants are then ranked or placed in the standings based on their winning percentage. The team/participant with the highest WP is ranked first, the team/participant with the next highest WP is ranked second, and so on, until all teams are placed in the standings. Below is an example of the final league standings for a summer softball league:

| Team | Wins | Losses | WP |
|------|------|--------|-----|
| Nick's TV | 11 | 2 | .846 |
| Gino's Menswear | 11 | 2 | .846 |
| Ben & Rose's Tap | 8 | 5 | .615 |
| Morton Insurance | 8 | 5 | .615 |
| Mr. T's Auto Body | 6 | 7 | .461 |
| Bea's Beauty Parlor | 5 | 8 | .348 |
| Swedish American Club | 3 | 10 | .230 |

Ties generally are broken by reference to the match or matches in which the entries met each other. For example, if Gino's Menswear had defeated Nick's TV in their earlier meeting, Gino's would be given the championship even though they both tied for first place by the same number of games.

## Practice Problems

Calculate the winning percentage for the following teams:

| Team | Wins | Losses | WP |
|------|------|--------|-----|
| Milwaukee Bucks | 25 | 18 | |
| Chicago Cubs | 82 | 30 | |
| Orlando Magic | 13 | 46 | |
| St. Louis Blues | 16 | 18 | |

## Games Behind The Leader

League participants who do not have the highest winning percentage are often interested in how close (or far behind) they are in relation to the first place team. To determine the number of games a team is behind the first-place team, use the following formula:

$$GB = [W_1 - W_x] + [L_1 - L_x] \div 2$$

Where:
GB = Number of games the team in question is behind the first-
     place team;
$W_1$ = Total number of wins by the first-place team;
$W_x$ = Total number of wins by the team in question;
$L_1$ = Total number of losses by the first-place team; and
$L_x$ = Total number of losses by the team in question.

The following example is provided to illustrate the calculations used to determine the number of games the Detroit Pistons are behind the Milwaukee Bucks. The Milwaukee Bucks have a win-loss record of 25 wins and 8 losses; the Detroit Pistons are 21-13. First, subtract the number of Piston wins from the number of Bucks wins (25 minus 21 equals 4). Next, determine the difference between the number of Bucks losses and Piston losses (8 minus 13 equals 5). Lastly, add the differences in wins and losses (4 plus 5 = 9) and divide by 2 to determine the total number of games the Detroit Pistons are behind the Milwaukee Bucks (4.5).

$$[25 - 21 = 4] + [8 - 13 = 5]$$
$$4 + 5 = 9 \div 2 = 4.5 \text{ Games Behind}$$

The league standing below shows the number of games the other teams are behind the Milwaukee Bucks

| Team | Wins | Losses | GB |
|------|------|--------|-----|
| Milwaukee Bucks | 25 | 8 | ----- |
| Detroit Pistons | 21 | 13 | 4.5 |
| Cleveland Cavaliers | 19 | 14 | 6.0 |
| Atlanta Hawks | 16 | 17 | 9.0 |
| Chicago Bulls | 10 | 23 | 15.0 |
| Indianapolis Pacers | 9 | 25 | 16.5 |

## Practice Problems

Using the information provided below in Table 3, produce the league's standings. Compute each team's winning percentage. Place the teams, in order of highest to lowest winning percentage, in a league standing. Next, calculate the number of games each team is behind (GB) the leader.

Develop a double round robin tournament for the following summer sand volleyball teams:

1. Dig It
2. Sand Pits
3. Spike and the Gang
4. In Your Face

5. Sand Witches
6. Bumpers
7. Vertically Challenged

Your facility has two sand courts. League play begins the first week in June and occurs on Tuesday and Thursday evenings. Matches start at 6:30 p.m. and 7:30 p.m. and last one hour.

At the end of the second round robin, the league standings look like this:

| | W | L | WP | GB |
|---|---|---|---|---|
| Sand Pits | 11 | 1 | | |
| Sand Witches | 10 | 2 | | |
| Dig It | 10 | 2 | | |
| Vertically Challenged | 9 | 3 | | |
| Bumpers | 6 | 5 | | |
| Spike and the Gang | 5 | 7 | | |
| In Your Face | 3 | 8 | | |

Determine the each team's winning percentage and games behind the leader.

## Points System

Another way of determining league standings is the point system. The point system is often used to place or rank league teams in sports that often end in a tie, such as hockey or soccer. Typically, 2 points are assigned to a team for each game won; 1 point for each tie game; and 0 points for games lost. Table 3 is an example of the point system for determining league standings.

TABLE 3

| Team | Wins | Losses | Ties | Points |
|---|---|---|---|---|
| Milwaukee Admirals | 25 | 18 | 3 | 53 |
| Peoria Chiefs | 22 | 20 | 4 | 48 |
| Quebec Nordiques | 12 | 30 | 4 | 30 |
| Chicago Blackhawks | 13 | 30 | 3 | 29 |
| St. Louis Blues | 6 | 38 | 2 | 14 |

## Practice Problems

Calculate the total points for the following teams listed in Table 4 and determine the final league standings.

TABLE 4

| Team | Wins | Losses | Ties | Points |
|------|------|--------|------|--------|
| Chicago Sting | 15 | 10 | 3 | |
| Milwaukee Wave | 22 | 3 | 1 | |
| New York Strikers | 17 | 5 | 4 | |
| Albuquerque Chilies | 13 | 13 | 1 | |
| Co. Springs Air Force | 6 | 20 | 2 | |

To stimulate spectator interest and encourage spirited competition throughout the entire match, officials of the Continental Basketball Association (CBA) have developed a point system to determine league standings. Three points are awarded to the game winner; and one point for the team with the highest score for each quarter of the game. In the event that the quarter score is tied, each team receives one-half point. For example, the Rapid City Thrillers and the LaCrosse Catbirds game had the following outcome (See Table 5):

TABLE 5

### EXAMPLE OF BASKETBALL POINT SCORING SYSTEM

| Team | Quarter Score | | | | Total Score | Points |
|------|------|------|------|------|-------------|--------|
| | 1 | 2 | 3 | 4 | | |
| Thrillers | 32 | 27 | 24 | 30 | 101 | 5 |
| Catbirds | 28 | 26 | 25 | 31 | 99 | 2 |

The Thrillers received 5 points since they won the game and had the highest score for quarters one and two; while the Catbirds received two points for having the highest score for quarters three and four.

## Statistics and Averages

Batting averages for softball and baseball are calculated by dividing the number of hits by the total number of times at bat.

Example:    Hits ÷ At Bats = Batting Average
31 ÷ 97 = .319

Pitching earned run averages (ERA) are determined by multiplying the number of earned runs by 9 and dividing this product by the individual's total number of innings pitched.  For events with regulation games of seven innings, the number of earned runs is multiplied by 7.

**Practice Problems**
Determine the batting and earned run averages for the following baseball players listed in Table 6:

TABLE 6

BATTING & EARNED RUN AVERAGES PRACTICE PROBLEM

| Player | Hits | At Bats | Average |
|---|---|---|---|
| Wade Boggs | 209 | 596 | |
| Jose Canseco | 174 | 610 | |
| Ricky Henderson | 152 | 588 | |
| Kirby Puckett | 207 | 634 | |
| Ryne Sandberg | 200 | 518 | |

A scoring average in basketball or any other sport is calculated by dividing the number of games played into the total points scored.  Table 7 contains an example of the 1991-1992 scoring averages for selected National Basketball Association players:

TABLE 7

BASKETBALL SCORING AVERAGES

| Player | Games | Points | Scoring Average |
|---|---|---|---|
| Michael Jordan | 79 | 2,410 | 30.9 |
| Karl Malone | 80 | 2,264 | 28.3 |
| Clyde Drexler | 82 | 2,312 | 28.2 |
| David Robinson | 78 | 2,083 | 26.7 |
| Chris Mullin | 80 | 2,112 | 26.4 |

**Point Systems**
A point system extends the scoring concept, and is cumulatively applied to all activities in the program.  The additional interest generated by these systems encourages participation in the program.  In each activity, points are assigned according to the order entries finish in the competition.  Points for each activity are added throughout the program to give entries an indication of their competitive positioning among other entries.  The entry which earns the most points at the end of the last programmed activity wins the all-around championship.

There are several different methods of the distributing points.  Some of the procedures are outlined in this section to illustrate the types of systems used in sports programming.

## Comparative High-Low Order

After an activity, each entry is assigned points according to its respective order of finish. The last place team receives 1 point; second from last, 2 points; third from last, 3 points; and so on. The first place team is awarded points equal to the number of entries. In some point systems, points are assigned only to the top four places. The number of points may be 4, 3, 2, 1; 100, 80, 60, 40, or any other four number combination. This method shifts the focus of the point system to winning one of the four top positions rather than consistent participation.

## Comparative Low-High Order

This point system is the reverse of the high-low method; the entry with the fewest points wins. The first-place entry receives 1 point and the last place entry receives points equal to the number of entries. Cross-country running competitions frequently use this method to determine team standings.

## Comparative Order Plus Entry Points

Entries receive points based on their order of finish as previously outlined and also receive points for entering the competition.

## Comparative Order Plus Game Points

Points are awarded for winning each game in addition to the points received for the order of finish. An arbitrary number of points may be established for winning each game such as 2, 4, 5, and so on.

## Combination System

Points systems can be created to include any or all of the previous distribution methods.

## Summary

A round robin tournament allows every entry to play every other entry regardless of record or ability and is often used to develop league schedules. The winner is determined by the team or individual with the highest percentage of matches won. To play a round robin tournament, you must have an equal amount of team positions. If you have an odd number of teams entered, for example, 5 teams, add one BYE and increase the number to six.

League standings are typically calculated to provide information on a team's win-loss records, winning percentage, ranking or place within the league, and the number of games behind the first-place team. A point system extends the scoring concept, and is cumulatively applied to all activities in the program. The additional interest generated by these systems encourages participation in the program.

# References

Byl, J. (1992). A round robin pyramid. *NIRSA Journal, 16*(2): 41-42.

Byl, J. (1991). Determining tournament suitability by the number of games per entry. *NIRSA Journal, 15*(2): 47-49.

Byl, J. (1990). Formalizing a ladder tournament: Revisiting Rokoskz's proposal. *NIRSA Journal, 15*(1): 41-43.

Rokoskz, F. (1989). How to formalize a ladder structure for tournament play. *NIRSA Journal, 13*(2): 14-18.

TABLE 4-2

## Winning Percentage Table

| Games Won | Games Lost | | | | | | | | | | | | | | |
|---|---|---|---|---|---|---|---|---|---|---|---|---|---|---|---|
| | 1 | 2 | 3 | 4 | 5 | 6 | 7 | 8 | 9 | 10 | 11 | 12 | 13 | 14 | 15 |
| 1 | .500 | .333 | .250 | .200 | .167 | .143 | .125 | .111 | .100 | .091 | .083 | .077 | .071 | .067 | .063 |
| 2 | .667 | .500 | .400 | .333 | .286 | .250 | .222 | .200 | .182 | .167 | .154 | .143 | .133 | .125 | .118 |
| 3 | .750 | .600 | .500 | .429 | .375 | .333 | .300 | .273 | .250 | .231 | .214 | .200 | .188 | .176 | .167 |
| 4 | .800 | .667 | .571 | .500 | .444 | .400 | .364 | .333 | .308 | .286 | .267 | .250 | .235 | .222 | .211 |
| 5 | .833 | .714 | .625 | .556 | .500 | .455 | .417 | .385 | .357 | .333 | .313 | .294 | .278 | .263 | .250 |
| 6 | .857 | .750 | .667 | .600 | .545 | .500 | .462 | .429 | .400 | .375 | .353 | .333 | .316 | .300 | .286 |
| 7 | .875 | .778 | .700 | .636 | .583 | .538 | .500 | .467 | .438 | .412 | .389 | .368 | .350 | .333 | .318 |
| 8 | .889 | .800 | .727 | .667 | .615 | .571 | .533 | .500 | .471 | .444 | .421 | .400 | .381 | .364 | .348 |
| 9 | .900 | .818 | .750 | .692 | .643 | .600 | .563 | .529 | .500 | .474 | .450 | .429 | .409 | .391 | .375 |
| 10 | .909 | .833 | .769 | .714 | .667 | .625 | .588 | .556 | .526 | .500 | .476 | .455 | .435 | .417 | .400 |
| 11 | .917 | .846 | .786 | .733 | .688 | .647 | .611 | .579 | .550 | .524 | .500 | .478 | .458 | .440 | .423 |
| 12 | .923 | .857 | .800 | .750 | .706 | .667 | .632 | .600 | .571 | .545 | .522 | .500 | .480 | .462 | .444 |
| 13 | .929 | .867 | .813 | .765 | .722 | .684 | .650 | .619 | .591 | .565 | .542 | .520 | .500 | .481 | .464 |
| 14 | .933 | .875 | .824 | .778 | .737 | .700 | .667 | .636 | .609 | .583 | .560 | .538 | .520 | .500 | .483 |
| 15 | .938 | .882 | .833 | .789 | .750 | .714 | .682 | .652 | .625 | .600 | .577 | .556 | .536 | .517 | .500 |

# TOURNAMENT DESIGN

   This chapter is devoted to the proper techniques and organization of sport programs including league scheduling, tournaments and races. Included in this section are numerous examples of leagues and tournaments as well as practice problems.

## Considerations Before Designing A Tournament
   Before designing a tournament several factors should be considered. Once the following questions have been addressed, it should be evident to the sports program planner the most suitable type of tournament, under the present circumstances.

   1. *Will a valid champion be determined?* In single elimination tournaments, each team does not have an opportunity to compete against the others words, therefore, the best team may not always win the tournament. A round-robin tournament format allows each team to compete head-to-head against each other. At the completion of the tournament, the team with the best record is declared the winner.

   2. *Will participants play an equal number of games?* Only the round robin tournament offers teams or participants the opportunity to play an equal number of games. If a team happens to lose their first game in the first round of a single elimination tournament, it would be their only game of the tournament. For teams that must travel a great distance and pay a high fee to participate in a tournament, the thought that they could play only one game could deter them from entering the tournament.

   3. *Will the activity be conducted on a team, individual or dual basis?*

   4. *Will interest be maintained throughout the tournament?* Double elimination and consolation tournaments provide another opportunity for teams or individuals to play after losing their first match, thereby maintaining participant and fan interest. If on-site concession revenues are important to the event organizer, it would be in her best interest to plan a tournament that keeps as many teams "alive" for as long as possible.

   5. *How much time will be required to complete the tournament?* The length of time available to complete the tournament will dictate the type and, along with the availability of human, physical and financial resources, the size of tournament to be held. For example, if the annual elementary school girls 8-team soccer tournament must begin on Saturday and end the next day, a single elimination tournament is recommended. The length of time assigned to complete a match and round within the tournament will also be influenced by the amount of time available. It is not uncommon for softball tournaments to limit the duration of a game to 50 minutes or seven

innings, whichever comes first. The team ahead at the end of the time period is declared the winner and advances in the elimination tournament.

6. *Are adequate facilities and equipment available?* Double and consolation tournaments are time-consuming if conducted on a single field and, depending upon when the tournament must be completed, may not be suitable tournament formats.

7. *How many winners are desirable?* A consolation tournament allows two teams to be declared winners, in contrast to round robin, single, double and semi-double elimination tournaments which produce a single winner.

8. *Is sufficient personnel available to officiate and supervise?* Depending upon the type and level of the sporting event produced, certified and experienced officials may be needed. For example, a coed recreational volleyball league may have a "call-your-own-violations" policy, requiring no game officials, while a women's' power volleyball tournament which qualifies teams for advanced competition may need as many as five game officials.

9. *Is evenly matched competition desirable?* Individual league and tournament participants particularly enjoy competing with players of like skills. A player does not enjoy a mismatch in which she is competing against another of superior ability; even the winner feels less than satisfied with the outcome of a mismatch. A Pyramid or King's Crown challenge tournament provide opportunities for players of relatively equal ability to compete and minimize mismatches.

10. *What are the revenue requirements?* If the tournament is intended to be profitable and concessions are available (i.e., food, beverages, souvenirs, etc.), double or consolation tournaments are recommended since an additional opportunity for play is available.

# CHAPTER FIVE
## Elimination Tournament Design

### Elimination Tournaments

The basic principle of all forms of elimination tournaments is the elimination, in each round of play, of half the field of contestants in that round. The winner of each match advances to the next round of play; the loser either is eliminated from further competition or is placed in some form of losers' bracket, in which the same principle of elimination holds.

Entries are paired for matches or games in accordance with the positions in which their names appear on a tournament chart or draw sheet. The elimination tournament has numerous variations all stemming from the basic principle of elimination under which either one or two defeats removes an entry from further competition.

### Single Elimination Tournament

The single-elimination tournament is a simple, quick method of determining a championship. In it, the loser of each match is eliminated from further play. Because of the speed with which entries are eliminated - half of the entire field in the first round, half of those remaining in the next round and so on until only one entry remains undefeated. The single elimination tournament is used when the number of contestants is large, the time for running the tournament is short, or the facilities are limited. Its use is not recommended where extensive participation is the main objective and the time element is not of prime importance.

Eight steps in developing an elimination tournament are outlined in the following pages:

STEP ONE: Determine Tournament Size

In choosing the number or size of an elimination tournament, you must choose a number which is an absolute power of 2. These are 2, 4, 8, 16, 32, 64.....the number you choose must be equal to or greater than the number of teams actually entered in the tournament.

Answer the following using STEP ONE

| Teams Entered | Tournament Size |
|---|---|
| 9 | _____ |
| 13 | _____ |
| 16 | _____ |
| 25 | _____ |
| 6 | _____ |
| 38 | _____ |

STEP TWO:  Determine Number of BYES

A BYE is a free pass given in the first round.  A BYE is not a game and will not better a team's record.  A simple formula to determine the number of BYES needed is as follows:
$B = T - N$

WHERE:  B = BYE
T = Tournament size
N = Number of teams actually in the tournament

With the following teams, calculate the number of BYES needed:

| Number of Teams In Tournament | BYES |
|---|---|
| 9 | _____ |
| 13 | _____ |
| 16 | _____ |
| 25 | _____ |
| 6 | _____ |
| 38 | _____ |

All BYES should be assigned in the first round.  One reason for this is that a match between an entry which has had a BYE during the preceding round and an entry which has just played in the preceding round is likely to be disadvantageous to the later. Since this is unavoidable, the BYE should take place as early as possible.  Another reason for scheduling BYES at the start is that interest, rivalry and relative importance of the matches increase as the tournament progresses, participants or spectators would not favor a format under which one or more teams sat out in one of the later rounds.

STEP THREE:  Determine Number of Games to be Played

The following formula should be used in determining the number of games played in a single elimination tournament.  This will assist you in knowing how many officials you might need, facility space and time.

G = N - 1

WHERE:  G = Number of Games; N = Number of teams in the tournament

With the following teams, calculate the number of games:

| Number of Teams In Tournament | Games |
|---|---|
| 9 | _____ |
| 13 | _____ |
| 16 | _____ |
| 25 | _____ |
| 6 | _____ |
| 38 | _____ |

STEP FOUR:  Back Number

Back numbering allows you to determine who is playing whom, who will receive the BYES and will make seeding the teams in the brackets easier.

To back number, divide the tournament size by 2.

In the case of a tournament with fifteen teams entered, the tournament size is 16 ÷ 2 = 8. Then number 1 through 8 on the left side of a page and 9 through 16 to their right beginning with 9 across from 8 and number up the page (See Below).

| | | | |
|---|---|---|---|
| 1. UNLV | | 16. | BYE |
| 2. Duke | | 15. | Texas |
| 3. Ohio State | | 14. | Virginia |
| 4. Syracuse | | 13. | Georgetown |
| 5. Arkansas | | 12. | UCLA |
| 6. North Carolina | | 11. | Michigan |
| 7. Indiana | | 10. | New Mexico State |
| 8. Illinois | | 9. | Princeton |

# 8 TEAM OR INDIVIDUAL TOURNAMENT

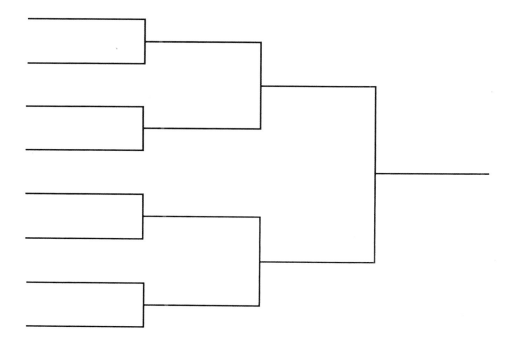

# 16 TEAM SINGLE ELIMINATION

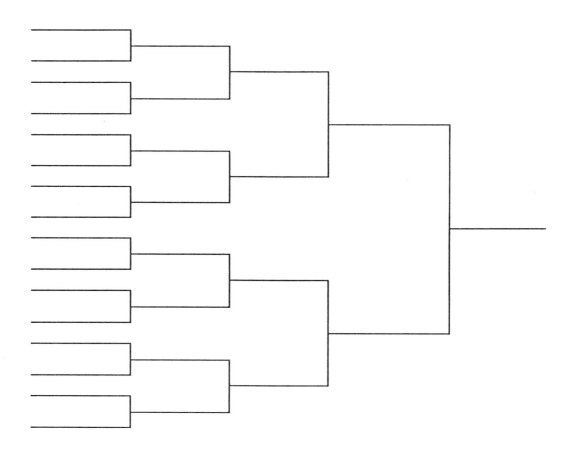

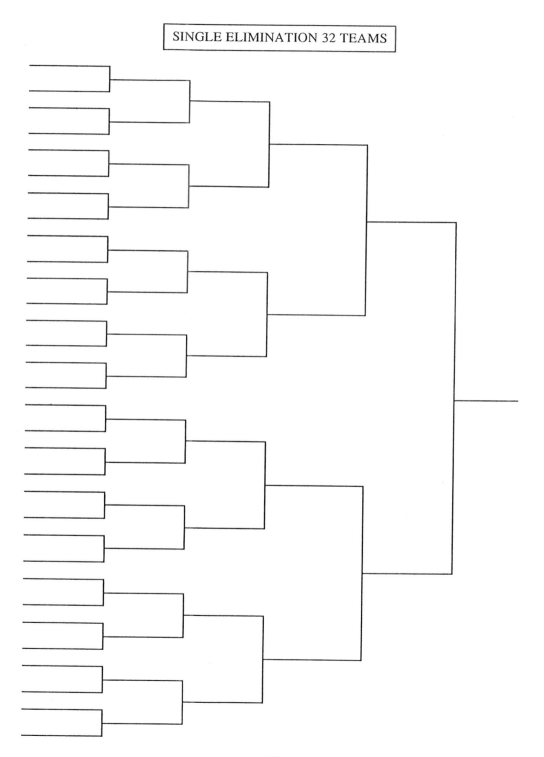

SINGLE ELIMINATION 32 TEAMS

Next, place the teams in order by record from 1 to 16 with BYES going at the end.

Practice STEP FOUR with the following information. Remember to use STEP TWO to determine number of BYES.

| Team | Record | Team | Record |
|------|--------|------|--------|
| Cardinals | 6-5 | Bears | 3-8 |
| Rams | 10-1 | Saints | 11-0 |
| Packers | 0-11 | Browns | 1-10 |
| Cowboys | 5-6 | Jets | 2-9 |
| Oilers | 7-4 | Seahawks | 8-3 |
| Lions | 9-2 | 49ers | 4-7 |

STEP FIVE: Draw Brackets

Brackets are two lines connected. The number or brackets you draw is equal to the tournament size. Then connect two of the horizontal lines with a vertical line, thereby establishing the first round brackets (See Figure 4-1).

Figure 1

### ROUND ROBIN SCHEDULING

#### ROUND ONE
| 1 - Braves | 8 - Expos |
|---|---|
| 2 - Brewers | 7 - Cardinals |
| 3 - Orioles | 6 - Cubs |
| 4 - Tigers | 5 - Mariners |

#### ROUND TWO
| 1 - Braves | 7 - Cardinals |
|---|---|
| 8 - Expos | 6 - Cubs |
| 2 - Brewers | 5 - Mariners |
| 3 - Orioles | 4 - Tigers |

#### ROUND THREE
| 1 - Braves | 6 - Cubs |
|---|---|
| 7 - Cardinals | 5 - Mariners |
| 8 - Expos | 4 - Tigers |
| 2 - Brewers | 3 - Orioles |

#### ROUND FOUR
| 1 - Braves | 5 - Mariners |
|---|---|
| 6 - Cubs | 4 - Tigers |
| 7 - Cardinals | 3 - Orioles |
| 8 - Expos | 2 -Brewers |

#### ROUND FIVE
| 1 - Braves | 4 - Tigers |
|---|---|
| 5 - Mariners | 3 - Orioles |
| 6 - Cubs | 2 - Brewers |
| 7 - Cardinals | 8 - Expos |

#### ROUND SIX
| 1 - Braves | 3 - Orioles |
|---|---|
| 4 - Tigers | 2 - Brewers |
| 5 - Mariners | 8 - Expos |
| 6 - Cubs | 7 - Cardinals |

#### ROUND SEVEN
| 1 - Braves | 2 - Brewers |
|---|---|
| 3 - Orioles | 8 - Expos |
| 4 - Tigers | 7 - Cardinals |
| 5 - Mariners | 6 - Cubs |

STEP SIX:  Seed Teams in Brackets

Seeding teams or individuals accomplishes two main goals:

1.  If seeded by record, it assures the teams or individuals with the best records will not play each other in the tournament for as long as possible.

2.  It will assure the BYES are evenly distributed. A BYE should not play a BYE if two teams or individuals are playing each other.

To seed the teams or individuals, place team one on the top line of the top bracket, place team two on the top line of the bottom bracket. Find the middle of the brackets. Place team four on the top line of the bracket just above the middle line and team three on the top line of the bracket just below the middle line. Now place the next odd number in the bracket above team four and the next even number in the bracket below team three. Continue to follow a pattern of odd-even until all brackets have a number on the top line. Once all the top lines of every bracket are filled, look back to STEP FOUR and fill in the corresponding number for all brackets.

When arbitrarily assigning first-round pairings, one of the considerations taken into account is to decide which entries to pair with seeded entires where seeded entries cannot be given BYES in the first round.

STEP SEVEN:  Number of Games to be Played

This is important for several reasons:  (1) the information will assist in the development of a time schedule; (2) certain games depend on other games being played before them; and  (3) BYE games need to be identified. Before playing a game, advance all teams playing a BYE. Games are numbered in progressive order.

STEP EIGHT:  Play the Tournament

Once all of the BYES are cleared, fill in the winners of games as they are completed.

## Seeding Tournament Teams or Individuals

When examining the participants in the tournament, it may be clear that some are significantly better than others. In such cases, the tournament "draw" should be seeded. Seeding the draw means manipulating or adjusting the order of first-round positions so that those with superior records do not meet in the early rounds of the tournament. While it may seem that the fairest way of determining pairings would be to randomly draw names out of a hat for first-round positions, consider that under this system some of the strongest entries might be scheduled with each other in the first round or might be placed so that they would meet each other in one of the early rounds. The result would be that some of the best entries would be eliminated at or near the beginning of the tournament, allowing weaker entries under the circumstances to advance and do better than their ability warrants. This would be unfair to superior contestants eliminated and would also detract from the overall interest in the tournament.

It is advised that the draw be seeded when there is known to be a significant difference in the respective strengths of the entries. In order to be effective and not subject to criticism, seeding must be done with extreme care by a person or persons having a good knowledge of the previous record of competitors. Generally, one entry is seeded for every four or eight entries, depending upon the number of entries having records which warrant their being seeded, and upon the size of the tournament.

Entries to be seeded are ranked in numerical order according to ability, first position being given to the entry with the highest ranking. Seeded entries are systematically distributed in the first round brackets so that, if accurate judgement has been used both in determining the entries to be seeded and in ranking these entries among themselves, and if no unexpected upsets occur, the final match will be between the best and second-best entries, the semi-finals will be between the third and fourth best, and the quarter-finals will be among the eight best entries, provided there are that many entries.

Teams or individuals are assigned to brackets based on a number of factors including league win-loss record, previous performance in the tournament, blind or random draw, "power" rankings, and tournament organization selection committee judgement. Where there are BYES and the draw is seeded, BYES usually are distributed first among the seeded entries. If there are fewer BYES than seeded entries, they should be given to these entries in the order of their respective rankings. The reason for giving BYES to seeded entires whenever possible is not to favor the stronger entries but to favor the weaker ones, as the more seeded entries having first-round BYES the more non-seeded entires will have a chance to play at least one match against competitors more or less in their own class.

Seeding teams based on league win-loss record places the first-place team against the last-place team in the first round (See section on single elimination tournament planning). Some tournaments will automatically assign the top seed to the team or individual who won the tournament the previous year. Some tournaments have restrictions on the type of teams or individuals allowed to participate. For example, a Class B fast pitch softball championship excludes those teams that have not attained that class status. Tournaments that allow any team or individual to enter are known as "opens." Without prior information regarding the skills and accomplishments of the registered participants, the tournament organizer may find it difficult to assign seeds. For example, a team from outside the community with a softball league win-loss record of 9-11 may be superior to another with a 11-3 record, depending on the "strength" or skill level of their respective leagues.

## Distributing Seeds

A popular system of distribution places seeded entries in the first round brackets according to the following arrangement:

Seed Number 1 at the top of the upper half
Number 2 at the bottom of the lower half
Number 3 at the top of the lower half
Number 4 at the bottom of the upper half

If a nonseeded draw should lead to unfavorable pairings in the first round, the draw is often adjusted, subject to the approval of the tournament committee. In a tournament bringing together participants from different areas, the pairing of contestants from the same area, particularly if they had to travel a great distance, would constitute an adjustment to the draw. Pairing entries that have played against each other on numerous occasions but have never or rarely met the other entries would also lead to an adjustment of the draw.

## Double Elimination Tournament

The double elimination tournament requires a much longer period of time to play than the single elimination. Each team must be defeated twice before being eliminated from further competition. As shown below, the championship bracket is carried on in the usual manner, with the defeated teams dropping into the losers' bracket. The teams that win out in both brackets are matched for the championship.

The EIGHT STEP method for running a single elimination tournament is also used for a double elimination tournament. Generally, double elimination tournaments are scheduled with 16 teams or less.

STEP ONE:  Determine Tournament Size
The process is the same as single elimination

STEP TWO:  Determine Number of BYES
The process is the same as single elimination

STEP THREE:  Determine Number of Games
The formula for a double elimination tournament is based on the single elimination formula and is as follows:

$$D = S \times 2 \text{ (or } + 1)$$

WHERE:  D = Number of double elimination games
S = Number of single elimination games

## 8-TEAM DOUBLE ELIMINATION TOURNAMENT

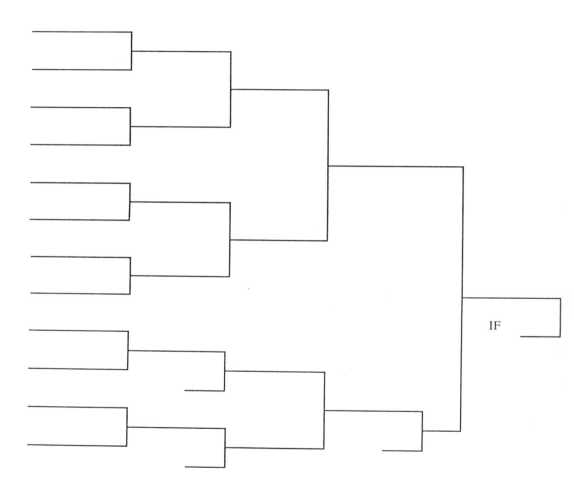

IF

## If Game

The reason there are two numbers for a double elimination tournament is because every team must lose twice before they are eliminated. Also , in the final game, there will always be one team that has lost one game and one team that has *not* lost a game. If the team that has lost one game loses the final game, the tournament is over. However, if the team that has never lost a game loses, another game must be played to determine the winner of the tournament. This game is known as the *IF* game. As a tournament programmer, make sure there are enough officials, time and space to play this game if needed.

STEP FOUR:  Back Number

The process is the same as in the single elimination tournament.

STEP FIVE:  Draw Brackets

The first part of drawing brackets is the same as in the single elimination tournament.  This is known as the winner's bracket (See Figure 3).

STEP SIX:  Seed Teams in Brackets

This process is identical to that of the single elimination tournament. Draw the brackets and seed teams by record.

STEP SEVEN:  Number Games to be Played

Advance teams playing BYES and drop the BYES down to their appropriate line in the loser's bracket.  Remember, BYES, whether in the winner's or loser's brackets do not count as games played.

STEP EIGHT:  Play Tournament

When dropping teams or BYES down in the first round, drop them down in order.  This is to insure teams that have already played each other will not play each other for as long as possible.  This rule applies so long as there is more than one team dropping down.

| DOUBLE ELIMINATION TOURNAMENT |
| --- |

Here is a double elimination practice problem:

ACTIVITY:    Junior Hockey
TOURNAMENT: Double Elimination
LOCATION:              Bobby Hull Ice Center ( 1 Rink)
FINANCIAL CONSIDERATIONS: Ice Maintenance, cost of officials
REGISTRATION FEES: TBA
REGISTRATION: 8 Teams
DATES: February 24 - TBD

Devise a double elimination tournament schedule for the top 8 teams in the Bobby Hull Junior Hockey League Tournament. Draw the tournament and include competitors, dates, and times. Seed teams for the double elimination tournament based on the league standings (below) and justify your scheduling decisions. Play out the tournament and place outcomes on the draw sheet.

| Name | W | L | T |
|---|---|---|---|
| Bauer Blades | 7 | 7 | 0 |
| Black Hawks | 3 | 10 | 1 |
| Mario Brothers | 10 | 2 | 2 |
| Penguins | 5 | 9 | 0 |
| The Great Ones | 6 | 7 | 1 |
| Black Ice | 13 | 1 | 0 |
| Big Zambonis | 11 | 2 | 1 |
| Montreal Canadians | 5 | 9 | 0 |
| High Stickers | 10 | 2 | 2 |
| Twin City Blues | 6 | 7 | 1 |
| Puck Lucks | 9 | 2 | 3 |
| Mighty Ducks | 11 | 1 | 2 |
| Slap Shots | 2 | 12 | 0 |
| Blue Line Specials | 8 | 6 | 0 |
| NY Rangers | 9 | 3 | 1 |

## Semi-Double Elimination Tournament

In a semi-double elimination tournament, competition begins on a double elimination format. Entires are paired according to elimination tournament procedures, with winners advancing in the winners' brackets and all first round losers playing in the losers' brackets. After this point, all games are played on a single elimination basis. The winners of the losers' and winners' divisions play for the championship. Figure 4 illustrates the back-to-back semi-double elimination draw sheet for 14 entries.

## Scoring Tournament

In scoring tournaments, the score rather than the outcome of head-to-head competition determines the winner. Example: Golf - the person with the lowest score wins the tournament. This type of tournament is often used to number of entries that could qualify for a scoring tournament or in conjunction with elimination tournaments.

## Contest

Another competitive format that provides a simple performance outlet is the contest that permits an individual to compare her skills against other entires. No interference by opponents is involved and a measurement or score determines the winner.

A basketball hot-shot contest represents this type of competition. Participants have one minute to shoot from designated spots on the court, each shot made from a spot receives a corresponding point value. Each entry does her best without having interference and the top score wins. Such contests are often run as special events, designed for individuals and unusually concentrates on one skill.

## Consolation Tournaments

There are various forms of consolation tournaments. All operate under the basic principle of giving the losers in certain rounds of the original elimination tournament a chance for further competition by placing them in losers' brackets or consolation rounds. Two defeats eliminate an entry from the tournament. Because all entries are given a chance to play at least two matches, the non-seeded draw is often employed.

The EIGHT STEP method used in running a single elimination tournament is also used for a consolation tournament. Just like a double elimination tournament, consolation tournaments are seldom used with more than 16 teams.

STEP ONE:  Determine Tournament Size
The process is the same as single elimination

STEP TWO:  Determine Number of BYES
The process is the same as single elimination

STEP THREE:  Determine Number of Games
The formula for a consolation tournament is based on the single elimination tournament and is as follows:

$$C = (S \times 2) - B$$
WHERE:        $C$ = Consolation tournament
              $B$ = Number of brackets for first round

STEP FOUR:  Back Number
The process is the same as single elimination

STEP FIVE:  Draw Brackets
Consolation tournaments are drawn by drawing a single elimination tournament in both directions (see Figure 5).  The first round winners are placed in the bracket to the right (winner's side) and the losers or BYES are placed in the brackets on the left (consolation side).

STEP SIX:  Seed Teams in Brackets
The process is the same as single elimination

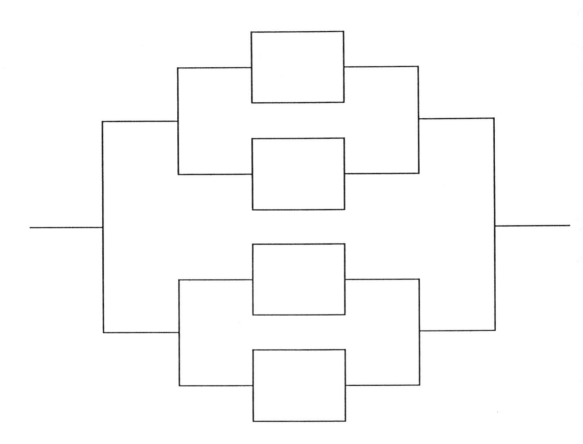

STEP SEVEN: Number Games to be Played

Number in order from top to bottom the brackets in the first round. Do not number BYE games. Then number the games to be played in the first round of the winner's side. Then the second round of the consolation side and the second round of the winners side. Continue the process until all the brackets without BYES are numbered. The last number should be placed in the final bracket on the winner's side.

STEP EIGHT: Play Tournament

Remember, after the first round, place the teams that lost or BYES in the consolation side and the winners in the winner's brackets. After this, any team that loses is out of the tournament. You will have two winners of the tournament.

## Summary

The basic principle of all forms of elimination tournaments is the elimination in each round of play, of half the field of contestants in that round. The winner of each match advances to the next round of play; the loser either is eliminated from further competition or is placed in some form of losers' bracket, in which the same principle of elimination holds.

Entries are paired for matches or games in accordance with the positions in which their names appear on a tournament chart or draw sheet. There are numerous forms of elimination tournaments with several variations stemming from the basic principle of elimination under which either one or two defeats removes an entry from further competition.

An important tournament management consideration is seeding the draw of entries, meaning manipulating or adjusting the order of first-round positions so that those with superior records do not meet in the early rounds of the tournament. The draw should be seeded when there is known to be a significant difference in the respective strengths of the entries. Generally, one entry is seeded for every four or eight entries, depending upon the number of entries having records which warrant their being seeded, and upon the size of the tournament.

Entries to be seeded are ranked in numerical order according to ability, first position being given to the entry with the highest ranking. Seeded entries are systematically distributed in the first round brackets so that, if accurate judgement has been used both in determining the entries to be seeded and in ranking these entries among themselves, and if no unexpected upsets occur, the final match will be between the best and second-best entries, the semi-finals will be between the third and fourth best, and the quarter-finals will be among the eight best entries, provided there are that many entries.

In single-elimination tournaments, the loser of each match is eliminated from further play. Because of the speed with which entries are eliminated - half of the entire field in the first round, half of those remaining in the next round and so on until only one entry remains undefeated. The single elimination tournament is used when the number of contestants is large, the time for running the tournament is short, or the facilities are limited.  Its use is not recommended where extensive participation is the main objective and the time element is not of prime importance.

In double elimination tournaments, each team must be defeated twice before being eliminated from further competition.  The championship bracket is carried on in the usual manner, with the defeated teams dropping into the losers' bracket.  The teams that win out in both brackets are matched for the championship.  In the final game, there will always be one team that has lost one game and one team that has *not* lost a game.  If the team that has lost one game loses the final game, the tournament is over.  However, if the team that has never lost a game loses, another game must be played to determine the winner of the tournament.  This game is known as the *IF* game.

In a semi-double elimination tournament, competition begins on a double elimination format.  Entires are paired according to elimination tournament procedures, with winners advancing in the winners' brackets and all first round losers playing in the losers' brackets.  After this point, all games are played on a single elimination basis.  The winners of the losers' and winners' divisions play for the championship.

Various forms of consolation tournaments exist but  all operate under the basic principle of giving the losers in certain rounds of the original elimination tournament a chance for further competition by placing them in losers' brackets or consolation rounds.  Two defeats eliminate an entry from the tournament.  Because all entries are given a chance to play at least two matches, the non-seeded draw is often employed.

Consolation tournaments are run like a single elimination tournament in both directions.  Like a double elimination tournament, consolation tournaments are seldom used with more than 16 teams.

# SPORT PROGRAMMING

## PRACTICE PROBLEMS

### CASE STUDY #1

ACTIVITY:  Men's NCAA Division I Basketball Tournament
TOURNAMENT:  64 Team Single Elimination
PARTICIPANTS:  Major College/University Basketball Teams Selected By NCAA
LOCATION:  Regional, National Sites
FINANCIAL STATUS:  NA
OTHER CONSIDERATIONS: Seeding

Devise a selection strategy and choose 64 teams to participate in this year's NCAA Division national men's basketball tournament. Determine team seeds and geographic location of tournament games. Play out the tournament. Justify your selection and seeding decisions.

### CASE STUDY #2

ACTIVITY:  Two-person Sand Volleyball
TOURNAMENT:  Double Elimination
PURPOSE:  Promote club, Special Event, Revenue
DATES:  JULY
LOCATION:  High Brow Athletic Club, 2 sand courts (No lights)
PARTICIPANTS:  Open Tournament (Men, Women and Co-Ed Divisions)
REGISTRATION:  10 Men's, 7 Women's, 9 Co-Ed Teams
FINANCIAL CONSIDERATIONS:  Profit Motive

Develop a double elimination sand volleyball tournament to accommodate the registered teams. Draw the tournament showing game sequences, competitors, times, and court assignments. Play out the tournament using fictitious team names.

### CASE STUDY #3

ACTIVITY:  NCAA Men's Division I Football
TOURNAMENT:  National Championship Tournament
PARTICIPANTS:  Major College and University Teams
LOCATION(S): TBA
OTHER CONSIDERATIONS: Seeding, Existing Bowl Format, Academic Schedules, Game and Television Revenues

Select teams to participate in the first NCAA Division I National Football Tournament. Determine the tournament format, team seeds and the geographic location of games, dates, and times and justify your scheduling decisions. Play out the tournament.

## CASE STUDY #4

ACTIVITY: Men's, Women's, Co-Ed Slow-Pitch Softball
TOURNAMENT: Single Elimination
LOCATION: University Fields
PARTICIPANTS: University Students, Faculty/Staff
REGISTRATION: Men's: 30; Women's: 39; Co-Ed: 13
FINANCIAL CONSIDERATIONS: Registration Fee, Cost of Umpires
Field Maintenance
DATES: April-May

Using existing school fields, devise a single elimination tournament schedule using fictitious teams. Draw and play out the tournament including competitors, field assignments, dates and times. Justify your scheduling decisions.

## CASE STUDY #5

ACTIVITY: Fall Youth Flag Football (Kids 12-14 years)
TOURNAMENT: Round Robin and End-of-Season Single Elimination
Tournaments
REGISTRATION: 19 Teams
LOCATION: Two Fields:
Csonka Field (Lights, good playing condition)
Elway Stadium (No lights, average playing field)
FINANCIAL CONSIDERATIONS: Officials - $10 per/game/per official

Using the above fields, devise league and tournament schedules using fictitious teams. Include game locations, dates, and times. Play out the league and show the final standings including wins, losses, ties, winning percentage, and games behind the leader. Seed the teams for the single elimination tournament and justify your scheduling decisions. Play out the entire tournament.

# CASE STUDY #6

ACTIVITY:  Girl's Basketball (Ages 13-14 years)
TOURNAMENT:  Round Robin and Consolation
PARTICIPANTS:  12 teams
LOCATION:  St. Mary's Church Gymnasium (1 Court)
FINANCIAL CONSIDERATIONS:  Officials - $5.00/Game
GAMES:         Saturday Mornings (8-12) and Tuesday Evenings (7-9 PM)

Devise league and tournament schedules using fictitious teams. Include game dates and times.  Play out the league and show final standings including wins, losses, winning percentages, and games behind the leader. Seed teams for consolation tournament play and justify your scheduling decisions.  Play out the tournament.

# SPORT PROGRAMMING

## SPORT ASSIGNMENT #1

You are the manager of the 32 lane King Pin Bowling Center. Twenty-eight teams have registered for your Wednesday Night Ladies League. League play begins the first Wednesday in November. Teams play three games each match.

Draw up the entire league schedule utilizing a round robin format. Include fictitious team names, lane assignments, games, dates and times. Hypothetically complete the league and detail the final standings. Justify your schedule.

At the conclusion of league play, a single elimination tournament occurs between the top eight teams. Draw up the entire tournament. Hypothetically play out the tournament.

## TOURNAMENT ASSIGNMENT #2

You are the recreation coordinator for Dugout City, South Dakota. Your community is sponsoring a Class D women's slow pitch consolation softball tournament in August. Dugout City has two softball diamonds, Babe Ruth and Babe Zaharias fields. Neither field has lights. This is a one weekend tournament with the first game not starting until 6:00 p.m. on Friday. The time limit for each game is fifty-five minutes.

Draw up the entire tournament including brackets for winners and consolation categories. Seed the teams based on their regular season records. Hypothetically complete the entire tournament. Each bracket should contain the names of the teams competing and the time, number and location of each contest played. Be able to justify your scheduling.

Team entries and regular season records are listed in Figure 6:

## FIGURE 6

| Team | Record | Team | Record |
|------|--------|------|--------|
| Bea's Beauty Parlor | 11-3 | American S&L | 8-6 |
| The Diet Center | 2-10 | Fanny Farmers | 3-12 |
| Andrea's Auto Body | 5-9 | White Sox | 5-9 |
| Dinah's Diner | 12-2 | Marty's Citgo | 7-7 |
| The Go-Go's | 8-8 | Gucci's | 4-12 |
| Mary Kay Cosmetics | 9-7 | A&P Groceries | 10-5 |
| Twins | 8-9 | Rose's Bar | 3-13 |

## SEMI DOUBLE ELIMINATION TOURNAMENT

Loser Gets to Lose Twice

Winners Only Lose Once

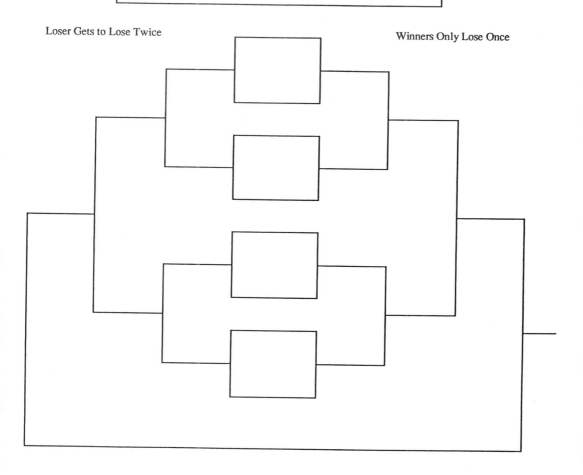

95

# 7 TEAM OR INDIVIDUAL ELIMINATION TOURNAMENT WITH IMPLIED BYES

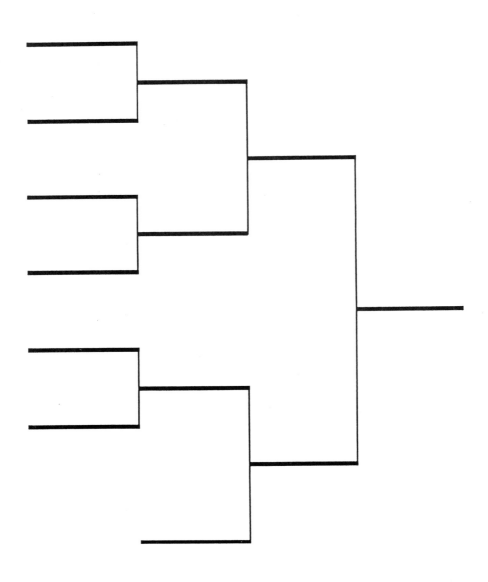

# CHAPTER SIX
## Challenge Tournaments

Challenge tournaments are designed to continually test a person's skills at the level they are playing. As skills increase, there will always be players whose skills are just a little better than yours to play against as well as players with skill a little below yours who will be challenging you. To facilitate this competition, many versions of challenge tournaments (a.k.a. motivational tournaments) have been developed such as ladder and pyramid tournaments. Challenge tournaments are set up on a time basis, generally 3-6 months in duration. The winner is determined by the person who is in the highest slot when the tournament ends. Generally this type of tournament requires no officials, however, considerable facility space and time are required. Challenge tournaments are widely used by health clubs and fitness centers for members involved in racquet sports such as racquetball, tennis, and squash. Rules should be made by the tournament manager to cover such issues as: How long does a person have to answer a challenge? Who can challenge whom? The following pages contain several challenge tournaments and suggestions of who can challenge whom, as well as selecting the right tournaments for the number of players participating.

### Ladder Tournaments

The ladder tournament is designed for small participant numbers, generally under ten. If the number of participants is more than ten, consider using another challenge tournament. Allow a player to challenge 2 positions above their own. In the example below, Mary could challenge John or Sally. If Mary wins, she takes their place.

### Pyramid Tournament

The pyramid tournament is much like the ladder tournament, the only differences being in the form of the tournament, and, in the number of entires on each level in the scale of rating, and in that both horizontal and vertical challenging are allowed.

The tournament format is designed, as the name of the competition implies, in pyramid shape, i.e., with one name at the top, two in the second row, three in the third, four in the fourth, etc. At the start of the tournament, no entry may challenge an entry on the next higher level without first winning a match from an entry on her same level. After this initial match has been won from a contestant on the same level, any entry may challenge any entry from the row directly above. As in the ladder tournament, positions in the pyramid are exchanged in the event the contestant on a higher level is defeated by one on a lower level.

RULE: Can challenge any player one level above.

# LADDER TOURNAMENT

| | |
|---|---|
| 1 | THURMAN |
| 2 | JANNETTE |
| 3 | MORRIS |
| 4 | DIANE |
| 5 | SARAH LEE |
| 6 | REGINALD |
| 7 | RUTH |
| 8 | DONALD |
| 9 | PHIL |

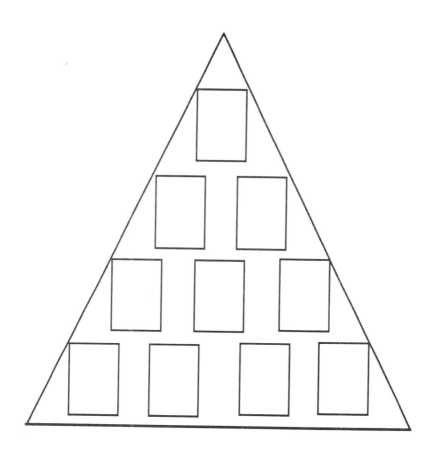

PYRAMID TOURNAMENT 10 ENTRIES

# CLOCK TOURNAMENT

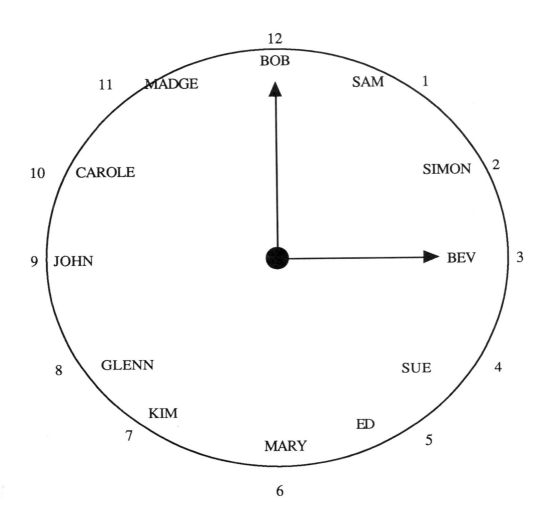

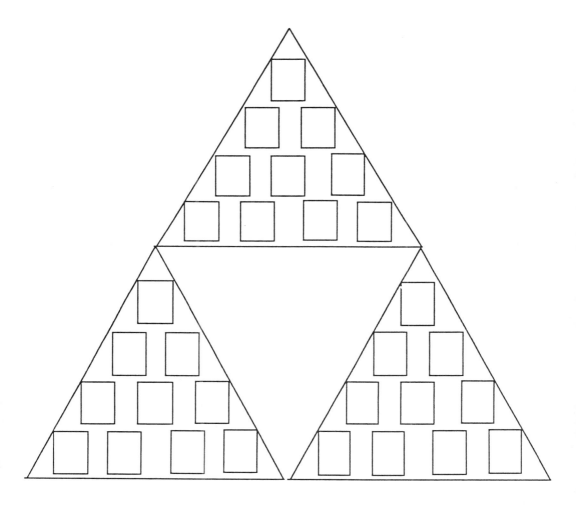

KINGS TOURNAMENT 66 ENTRIES

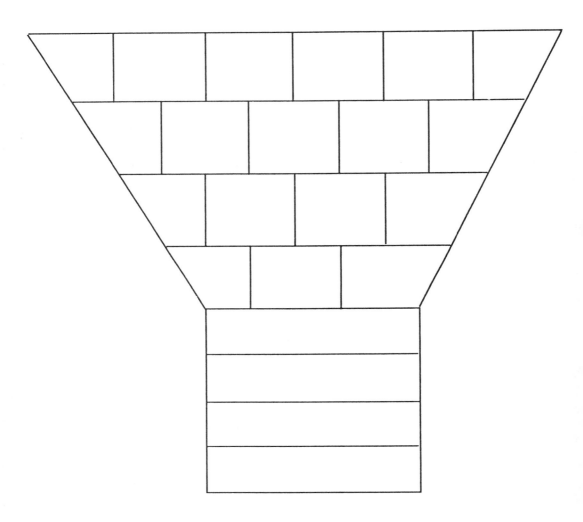

FUNNEL TOURNAMENT
22 ENTRIES

## Clock Tournament
12 participants
RULE: Challenge player one level ahead of your position.

## King or Crown Tournament
The king's tournament is an expanded version of the pyramid tournament in which the tournament format consists of several pyramids which are placed on various levels of a scale or rating. Challenging is vertical within a given pyramid, horizontal between pyramids, the object to get to the top, or the king's position in the highest pyramid.

RULES:
Challenge just as in pyramid tournament.
Top of pyramids can challenge any player on bottom line of pyramid directly above them.

## Funnel Tournament
Funnel tournaments combine the features of a ladder and pyramid tournament. Players in the top section follow pyramid rules; the bottom four players advance to the lowest position using the ladder rules. The main objective of this tournament is to filter through the funnel to the lowest place. In Figure 16, Wilson is the winner if the position is held at the end of the tournament.

## Spider Web
The spider wed tournament is conducted according to the rules of the pyramid tournament. Figure 17 illustrates a spider web tournament for 19 entries. The object of the spider web tournament is to advance to the center and maintain that position. A drawback is that the player in the middle must accept numerous challenges from the six players occupying adjacent positions. To minimize the constant pressure placed on this player, it is recommended that players challenge someone on their own level before challenging the center position.

## Record Board Tournament
The record board tournament is one in which participants do not compete directly against one anther but challenge scores or records posted on a board. The name, date and performance of a competitor who breaks one of the listed records is placed in the appropriate position on the board, with the other names adjusted in descending order and the last name dropped from the board. This format provides excellent motivation for running, swimming, bicycling, weightlifting and other events graded on a time, distance or weight measure. If a contestant runs 10K in 32 minutes and 11 seconds, his or her time is recorded in second place, Mary and Steve shift to third and fourth, and John is dropped from the board.
Bowling and golf are also well-suited for the record board format. For example, names of the top 10 bowlers and their respective scores can be listed on the board. A bowler who bowls the third highest score moves into

third place on the board and all the bowlers below her are moved down one position with the last bowler being removed from the board. Bowlers may bowl at any time during the tournament in an attempt to gain a position on the board.

# Sport Rules and Regulations

Sport rules and regulations have been established to serve as a guide for safe, fair and enjoyable participation. Engagement in recreational sports is voluntarily chosen and participants should understand and support the limitations established by the rules. Sport rules apply specifically to each individual activity. For additional information on the specific rules for a sport of interest, contact the sport's governing body or federation. A partial list of sports organizations can be found in Appendix A.

This section presents information on rules and procedures for sport programs including postponements and re-scheduling, forfeits, rule infractions, and handicap scoring. Also featured are unique sport formats and variations of traditional sport rules intended to make play more equal, safe and enjoyable. The information presented is intended to aid sport organizers in effective management.

## Sport Program Management Considerations
*Postponements and Re-scheduling*

Postponed matches are inevitable in sports programming, particularly because of inclement weather. When weather causes several nightly softball schedules to be postponed, it is possible to make-up the games by playing doubleheaders of shorter durations. For example, a five-inning double header may be scheduled to make up two weeks of postponed games. When scheduling outdoor sport matches, account for make-ups.

*Forfeits*

A sports program with no forfeits indicates an efficiently administered program and enthusiastic, satisfied participants. Most participants look forward to playing their matches and are disappointed when their opponents fail to show. Numerous forfeits serve to undermine the spirit of the sports program and ultimately will lead to a decreased number of entries. Some leagues will bar an entry from further participation after 3 forfeits. Other organizers require forfeit fees when entries register for league or tournament participation. Regardless of the policy, participants should be briefed on the penalties, if any, for forfeits, prior to play.

*Rule Infractions*

Depending on the nature of the sport, its format, and purpose of the program, the following may be considered rule infractions for sport participation.

1. Playing for more than one team in the same league.

2. Playing under an assumed name.

3. Misrepresenting a score

4. Using players not eligible for the program

5. Unsportsmanlike conduct

Management methods used for violations of the above infractions may include:
1. Forfeiture of the game or games in which the ineligible player participated.

2. Removal of team or individual points from the activity in which the player was involved.

3. Disqualification of the individual from participating in any agency sport for a specified period of time such as one season or one year.

4. Barring teams or organizations from competition for a specified period of time

5. Indefinite suspension from the program if violations are repeated.


## Variations of Traditional Rules In Sports

Tillman (1973: 112) explains the challenges facing sport planners. "The job of the programmer is not just to throw out the ball and stand back. The goal of perfect play, total participation fulfillment, is a demanding, creative, scientific, and perceptive challenge, not the least of which is the constant need to equalize competition." The following is a partial list of rule adaptations to traditional sports. The in many cases, sport programmers will alter rules to make play more closely matched, enjoyable for participant, and safer.

*Softball*
Balls and Strikes - To speed play, some leagues and tournaments limit 2 strikes and the batter is out; 3 balls and the batter is "walked" and awarded first base.

Foul Ball Strike Out - Another rule relative to balls and strikes is the foul ball out rule. Contrary to professional baseball rules where a batter may foul off an unlimited number of pitches and still continue the at-bat, some leagues require that if the batter has two strikes and the next ball struck is foul, the batter is out.

No Slide Rule - To minimize the number and severity of leg, ankle and knee injuries, some leagues/tournaments prohibit sliding into bases.

Strike Mat - To relieve the burden and/or discrepancy that may exists when umpires call balls and strikes, some leagues/tournaments use a strike mat; If the pitched ball meets a minimum arc or ball height requirement and hits the mat without touching the batter's bat, it is a strike; any pitched ball that is misses the mat is called a ball.

Force-out Line - Leagues that allow base sliding but also are concerned with participant safety have instituted a Force-out line along the path between third base and home plate, approximately thirty-feet from third base.

Coed Softball - Females and males alternate within the batting order. Males receive two bases if walked.

*Tennis*
Ten game matches rather than 6 game sets and two-out-of-three sets to determine the match winner.
Team Tennis - Games are played to 4 points - no deuce games. A match is comprised of 10 games with no tie-breakers.

Sheet Volleyball - An opaque white sheet is draped over the standard volleyball net to hide the opposing team's movements.

Coed Volleyball - If two or three teammates combine to strike the ball over the net, at least one of the players must be female

World Bicycle Polo Association - Mountain bicycles are substituted for horses.

Coed Basketball - Males cannot play within the "three-second lane" or "paint."
Six-Foot and Under League

## Handicap Procedures

Handicapping is a method of equalizing competition between opponents of unequal ability. In some cases, participants with lesser ability simply do not enter competition unless there is a reasonable to defeat some of the other competitors. A handicap system "levels the playing field" by providing an artificial advantage for the entries of lesser ability, enabling them to compete on an equal basis with entries of greater ability. A non-handicapped sports event is referred to as "scratch." There are several methods of handicapping. For tennis singles, the better player may be required to cover the entire doubles court while the opponent plays within the singles boundaries. Bowling and golf are sports that commonly use handicap systems. A guide to determining golf handicaps is located in Table 1.

## Other Tournament Formats

The Bagnall-Wild tournament selects second and third place winners. The format is used primarily in wrestling meets or other sports where importance is placed

### *Golf*

Golf competition may be organized several ways, several of which are discussed in this section. For precise handicapping, the United States Golf Association (USGA) method should be used (See Table 2).

### Match Play

Match play involves head-to-head competition between two players. Medal or stroke play is the number of times a player attempts to strike the ball to complete a round. The total number of strokes is posted for each player and the one with the lowest total is the winner.

For team competition, groups may enter any number of players. Each player's score is recorded at the end of the round, and the total of the four lowest scores makes up the team total; the team with the lowest combined score is declared the winner.

### Medal or Stroke Play

Match play involves competition between two players, each attempting to win a greater number of holes by taking the fewest number of strokes per hole. If the score is posted as 2 up, it means that one player won two more holes than her opponent. If the score is 3 and 1, it means a player has won three holes more than her opponent with only one hole left to play. If a tie results after 18 holes of play, additional holes are played until the tie is broken.

### Naussau Scoring Method

This scoring method pairs the ranked players of each team against each other. Three points are awarded for each match based on the number of holes won. One point is awarded to the winner of the first nine holes, one point to the winner of the second nine holes, and one point to the player who wins the greatest number of holes for a complete 18-hole round.

### Innovative Sports Programs

1. Organize a system similar to professional sports league in which teams are allowed to draft and trade players.

2. Establish a tournament for the last place teams in each league

3. Develop a triple or quadruple elimination tournament

4. Schedule the finals of a free throw, three point or super-shooter contests during the half-time of a high school or college/university varsity game.

5. Outdoor winter sports festivals are popular in communities where snow and ice are consistently available each winter, Activities may include cross-country skiing, biathlon, showshoeing, ski relays, speed skating, broomball, hockey, and dog sled racing.

## Sports Program Planning Blueprint

Before developing a recreational or competitive sports program, a thorough plan or "blueprint" should be devised. Table 1 contains the the essential elements of a program blueprint.

TABLE 1

SPORTS PROGRAM PLANNING BLUEPRINT

1. Sponsoring agency; including individual in charge, their title, address, telephone and fax numbers.

2. Program title and a brief description of what you are planning including date(s) time(s) and location(s).

3. Target Market
Briefly describe the population to be served including their geographic, demographic, and socio-economic profiles.

4. Program Goals

5. Objectives
     a. Operational
         i. Checklist including time-line
     b. Performance

6. Logistical Arrangements
     a. Facilities and Location Description (Diagram/Map)

7. Equipment and Supplies

8. Contractual Agreements

9. Budget
     Propose a line-item budget necessary for an effective program. Upon completion of the program, submit an actual cost budget.

10. Volunteers

11. Market Plan
      a. Product/Service    b. Price
      c. Distribution       d. Promotion

12. Contingency Plan
      What will be done if the tournament meets inclement weather; if the referees scheduled do not show up for their game; if darkness prevents the completion of the championship game; if a formal complaint is made by a team regarding the quality of officiating? The astute sports programmer constantly asks herself, "What if...?" during the planning stages and seeks ways to answer the question.

13. Risk Management Plan

14. Program Evaluation

15. References

## SCHEDULING

Careful consideration should be given to the following when developing schedules:

1. Available equipment and facilities

2. Number of teams or individuals entered

3. Time allotted for the program

4. Number of matches required to complete the schedule

5. Conflicts with other activities

6. Allowance for postponements due to inclement weather

7. Seeding entries

      Scheduling a team to play the same night each week is an important consideration. Participants are permitted to arrange other activities accordingly. Sooner or later, some entries will be required to play at different times in order to meet winners of other divisions in the play-offs.
      It is important to set specific times, dates and locations for tournament matches or league games on the schedule.

## ENTRY FORMS

Entry forms should request information necessary to complete a schedule. The following list contains the types of items to be included on entry forms:

1. Name of activity/program

2. Name of entrant

3. Manager's or captain's name, address, telephone and fax numbers

4. Specified hours participants prefer and/or cannot participate

5. Date of entry

6. Alphabetical listing of the team roster

7. Initials of staff registrar

Figure 3 contains an example of an entry form for a softball tournament. Figure 4 provides an example of a 3-on-3 basketball tournament. Examples of registration forms for running races may be found in Chapter 9.

## FIGURE 3

## CASE STUDY

The following case study has been included to illustrate the financial considerations in programming a recreational sport event.

Program: Format - 16 team double elimination softball tournament
Duration - Play begins Friday night, continues Saturday morning and concludes Sunday afternoon

### Direct Costs

| | | |
|---|---|---:|
| Field Maintenance | $10/game x 31 games = | $ 310 |
| Awards | First place - 12 engraved bats @ $7 = | $ 84 |
| | Second place - 12 specialty softballs @ $4 = | $ 48 |
| Umpires | 2 umpires/game x 31 games = 62 umpire games x $20 = | $1240 |
| Balls 3/game x 31 games =93 balls @ $2 = | | $ 186 |
| Promotional Materials | | |
| | Flyers, advertisements, posters, banners | $ 450 |
| Electricity (field lights) 6 night games @ $12 = | | $ 72 |
| Score book | | $ 4 |
| Total Direct Costs | | $2394 |

**Indirect Costs**
Tournament Coordinator
$25,000 (annual salary) ÷ 52 weeks = $480
12 weeks of tournament work x
10 hours/week = 120 hours or 3/40 hour weeks x $480 =

<u>$1440</u>

**Total Costs**                                                              $3834
Tournament Fees/Team to Break Even
16 teams - $240
14 teams - $274
If the event is to break even, team registration fees must be between $240 and $274 depending upon the number of teams entered. Donations or local sponsorships can be obtained to reduce direct costs.

Tournament or game rules are sometimes printed on entry forms. It is advised to print a separate supplemental sheet containing rules for entries to take with them after completing the registration form. Entries can be notified through schedules in the mail or newspaper. Schedules should also be placed at the agency headquarters and areas where the matches take place. There are no acceptable excuses for forfeits if schedules are carefully made and entries properly notified.

## Qualifying Rounds or Heats

A large number of entries may be more manageable by staging one or more qualifying rounds or heats prior to final competition. This practice is typically used in track, swimming, golf and bowling. In track and swimming, only the best performers advance to the finals. In golf and bowling, numerous players play in the qualifying rounds, but only the top 32 or 64 players or those who are under a specific cutoff score continue in the tournament.

## References

Byl, J. (1990). *Organizing Successful Tournaments*. Champaign, Illinois: Human Kinetics.

Gaskins, D. (1992). A three point plan for reducing forfeits in intramural sports. *NIRSA Journal*, *16*(2): 44-48.

Glakas, B. A. (1991). Teaching cooperative skills through games. *Journal of Physical Education, Recreation, and Dance*, *62*(5): 28-30.

Kozlowski, J. C. (1991). NRPA Law Review. *Parks and Recreation*, *26*(8): 20-23, 70.

Kuga, D. J. (1991). Improve your intramural program: Evaluate! *Strategies*, *15*(2): 12-15.

Mood, D. P., Musker, F. F., & Rink, J. E. (1991). *Sports and Recreational Activities for Men and Women*. St. Louis: Mosby Year Book.

Mueller, P. & Reznik, J. W. (1979). *Intramural-Recreational Sports: Programming and Administration* (Fifth Edition). New York: John Wiley & Sons.

Reetz, S. (1992). A viable alternative: A 4 on 4 passing tournament. *NIRSA Journal*, *16*(2): 34-35.

*Sports Market Place* (1991). Richard A. Lipsey (Editor). Princeton, NJ: SportsGuide, Inc.

Sylvia Worth, Editor. (1990). *Rules of the Game*. New York: St. Martin's Press.

Sports Sponsorship: Its Strictly Business. *Athletic Business*, (October 1, 1990) 14, 1: 59.

Seibert, G. Recreation vs. Sports Programs for Kids. *Fitness Management* (June 1, 1991) 7,1: 26.

Smith, S. R. & Carron, M. F. (1990). Comparison of competition and cooperation in intramural sports. *NIRSA Journal, 15*(1): 41-47.

# CHAPTER SEVEN
## FINANCING RECREATIONAL SPORT

INTRODUCTION

*Program Budget*

A **program budget** is a written plan for a specific program (i.e., softball tournament) an  agency conducts, reflecting the program's revenues and expenditures for the next calendar or fiscal year. Figure 1 contains a financial balance sheet useful in sport programming.

The first step in developing a program budget is to review and determine all sources of revenues.  Typical revenue sources for sport programs include registration fees, gate receipts, concessions, parking, and programs.

Step two involves projecting all sources of possible program expenditures.  These expenditure estimates can be based on past program experience and on anticipated expenditure changes in the program.

Lastly, the program budget is submitted to the agency manager or chief executive officer and/or board of directors for approval.  Who reviews the program budget is generally dependent upon the scale and nature of the organization.  Revenue and expenditures may be adjusted during the review process to generate an acceptable and realistic budget plan.

FIGURE 1

## SPORTS PROGRAM BALANCE SHEET

**REVENUES**

| | |
|---|---|
| Agency appropriations | $_____ |
| Participant Registration Fees _____ @ $_____ / Participant = | $_____ |
| Admission Fees _____ @ $_____ / Spectators = | $_____ |

Concessions
      Food/Beverages      $_____
      Souvenirs      $_____
      Other      $_____

Sponsorships      $_____

Donations      $_____

TOTAL REVENUES      $_____

**EXPENDITURES**

Services -Personal      $_____

Services - Contractual      $_____

Commodities      $_____

Other Expenses      $_____

Capital Outlay      $_____

TOTAL EXPENDITURES      $_____

## MAJOR EXPENDITURE CLASSIFICATIONS

The information presented in this section discusses in detail the various expenditure classifications listed in Figure 1.
SUBTOTAL

I.    Services -Personal

    $_____

Personal services involve salaries and wages paid to persons employed by the organization.

II.    Services - Contractual

Contractual services involve work performed for the organization through agreement or contract by persons other than employees, as well as the provision of equipment and furnishing of commodities under agreement.

A. Communication and Transportation

$_____

These expenses include the cost of postage, telephone, fax, freight, express and expenses for transporting persons and reimbursement of expenses incurred by staff for use of their own personal vehicle.

B. Printing and Advertising

$_____

These expenses include all charges for printing including advertising and printing of legal notices, and expenditures for photocopying, photography and binding.

C. Professional Services

$_____

These expenses include all charges incurred for any accounting function such as data processing, cost of engineering and architectural consultants, and other professional services such as legal or financial consultants.

D. Utilities

$_____

Charges for heat, light, power, sewer, and water furnished by utility enterprises.

E. Insurance

$_____

These expenses include premiums paid for fidelity bonds, worker's compensation and unemployment compensation insurance, insurance on buildings, equipment and land, liability and those premiums paid for employee's medical and life insurance policies.

F. Repairs

$_____

Include all repair expenses of a contractual nature for buildings, structures, walks, roads and equipment, and the costs of service contracts for equipment.

G. Maintenance Services

$_____

These charges include field preparation and maintenance, janitor, waste removal, snow removal, pest control and other services required to maintain sports operations.

I. Other Contractual Services

$_____

These charges include all other services of a contractual nature that are not included in other categories.

III. Commodities

This group of expense includes both supplies and materials.

A. Supplies

$_____

A supply is a commodity that is consumed, impaired or warn out in a reasonably short period of time. Such supplies include stationery, food, fuel, clothing, pool chemicals, fertilizer, ballfield chalk, medical and cleaning supplies.

B. Materials

$_____

Materials are items of a more permanent nature that may be combined or converted to other uses. Materials include lumber, paints, iron or other building materials, masonry and road materials, fiber products, trees and shrubs, repair parts.

IV. Other Expenses

$_____

Other expenses are those charges incurred that are not commodities or contractual in nature. They include items such as interest expenses paid for the use of money or capital, payments of legal claims and judgements against the recreation and park sports organization, refunds of overpayments received or when a sports program with a registration fee is cancelled.

V. Capital Outlay

$_____

Includes charges for land, equipment, buildings, structures and fixed improvements. Equipment here includes movable items that, when used, show little impairment or change and have a definite period of usefulness. Furniture, machinery, motor vehicles and tools readily fall under this classification.

## Classification

| | | | |
|---|---|---|---|
| I. | Services -Personal | $ | _____ |
| II. | Services - Contractual | $ | _____ |
| III. | Commodities | $ | _____ |
| IV. | Other Expenses | $ | _____ |
| V. | Capital Outlay | $ | _____ |

TOTAL EXPENDITURES                    $_____


## Price Strategies in Sport

There are several pricing strategies employed in the delivery of sport services. This section provides a brief summary of the most common pricing strategies.

### Break Even Pricing

Break even pricing involves charging participants the full unit cost to produce the service.

Fixed Costs: overhead, stadium rental, taxes, office equipment, etc.
Variable Costs (wages, materials, concessions, etc.)
Total Cost = FC + VC
Total Revenue = Price x Quantity

### Cost-Plus Pricing

Cost-plus pricing includes a profit margin on top of the full unit cost to deliver the sport service. The service delivery cost, plus the desired profit, equals price charged to the customer.

### Price Penetration

Price penetration involves pricing services in the lower range of expected prices to increase quantities purchased. This technique is often used when new products or services are introduced.

### Skim Pricing

Involves pricing inelastic services high to generate more revenue. Some sport services are in such high demand that many will pay higher prices in order to receive the benefits of consumption. Examples of sport service providers using skim pricing include stadium owners charging premium prices for luxury box suites.

## Discount Pricing

Discount pricing offers a way to generate untapped revenue from market segments that are not able, for whatever reasons, to pay the full market value for a good or service. By offering some services at a discount, the sport manager will maximize facility use and realize varying levels of revenue from numerous sources.

A relatively new discount pricing strategy is to build "fences" that allow consumers to logically segment themselves into an appropriate rate category based upon their consumption behavior (i.e., needs, willingness to pay, usage, etc.). The airline industry's advance purchase requirements and Saturday night stay-over are examples of price fencing. "A price fencing strategy affords price-sensitve users lower rates in exchange for decreased flexibility. On the other hand, full-rate customers can use the services at traditionally higher demand times." (Cato & Crotts, 1993)

| Rate Fence for a Municipal Sport Complex | | | | |
|---|---|---|---|---|
| Price | Requirements | Day of Week | Time of Day | Users |
| 50 cents | 14-day advanced reservation | Off peak | Off peak | Groups |
| $1.25 | None | Off peak | Off peak | Retirees, Unemployed, Children |
| $2.50 | None | Peak times | Peak times | Price-insensitive individuals |

## Nonresident Fees and Charges

Most citizens do not feel that fee collection constitutes double taxation. The importance of the definition of a nonresident varies,but if nonresidence fees are to be collected, then the boundaries must be easily defined to be able to levy the fee. When debating whether to charge nonresidence fee, local government-sponsored sport and recreation agencies should consider the following:

+ Fee programs can subsidize non-fee programs
+ Fee programs serving special clientele are not necessarily a tax burden to everyone.
+ Five percent or less of the population is negatively affected by user fees (nationally).
+ The public is no longer willing to provide unlimited tax dollars for public recreational sport programs.
+ In local government-sponsored recreational sport, there is a growing feeling that activities should be supported by those who use them, rather than by the public.

+ Doubling fees can work where teams have sponsors.
+ Doubling fees can kill a program where individual team members supply the money.
+ Fee charges require some experimentation and fine-tuning.

+ Advance notice and gradual fee increases are essential for public acceptance.

+ Some facilities will fail to be financially self-sustaining, but the total mission of the agency becomes financially reasonable when a facility or program attracts revenue or support in other areas.

+ Nonresidents can help support programs that have capacity at little or no additional expense.

## Equity Pricing

One of the most serious issues related to sport and recreation fees and charges is the question of equity. The question is whether people are deprived of recreational sport services because they cannot afford the fee. There are a number of techniques that are used by recreational sport agencies to reduce the user fee impact on those that cannot afford to pay. These techniques include:

1. Reduced rates for selected groups e.g., handicapped, low income/welfare, children, and elderly.
2. Waive fees for some individuals.
3. Provide scholarships using contributions from local businesses or citizen groups (sponsors can help those with lower incomes).
4. Adjust fee structure according to income level of neighborhood.
5. Allow extended payment schedules.
6. Provide work exchange programs in lieu of fees.

## PRICING SPORT SERVICES

McCarville (1993) offers several pricing principles and key tips to successful pricing in sport and recreation:

Principle One - Participants Seek Fairness in Pricing

Tip #1 - Price is considered most appropriate for those activities that clearly benefit only the participant.

Tip #2 - Use other providers' prices as a guide when developing new price levels.

Tip #3 - If you must increase your prices, do so in small increments on a regular basis.

Tip #4 - Tell customers how much it costs to provide the program they are about to enjoy.

Principle Two -Consumers Seek Value
Tip #1 - Focus on benefits to be enjoyed through purchase.
Tip #2 - Assign program names that focus on the benefits of participation.
Tip #3 - Ensure your clients know how they benefit from paying a fee.
Tip #4 - Compare new programs to well established and valued alternatives.
Tip #5 - Tell the world how wonderful you and your staff are.
Tip #6 - Stress the convenience element in all your programs.
Tip #7 - Offer liberal refund policies to reduce uncertainty.

Principle Three - Consumers Seek Choices
Tip #1 - Always provide price alternatives
Tip #2 - Give the consumer choices as to the kind of price to be paid (i.e., box seats, mezzanine, upper grandstand, bleachers)

## CASE STUDIES IN SPORT PRICING

1. The ISU Athletic Department is contemplating a change in its men's home basketball single game ticket price structure so that price is directly linked to the quality of one's court view, and to make attendance more affordable to families. Attached is the current price structure for ISU men's basketball home games at Redbird Arena. What changes will you make to this price plan and with what rationale? Who will receive price discounts to the full price of a game ticket and why?

2. The first Viet Nam Memorial Running Race will be held in Bloomington, IL this May. The purpose of this event is to raise money for the Viet Nam Veterans Scholarship Fund, which provides educational assistance to dependants of war veterans. The event features a half-marathon race, 5 mile race and a non-competitive 5 kilometer walk. Individual and team competitions are available in both the half-marathon and 5 mile races. Over 500 people are expected to participate. Pre-race registration will be accepted until May 20th and is $5 less than race day registration.
What are the fixed costs associated with this event?
Identify several variable costs.
Develop a registration fee structure and justify your decisions. Is there a going rate for running race registrations?
Will each race have a different price? Who will receive price discounts and why?

3. The ISU Athletic Department is contemplating a change in its men's home football single game ticket price structure so that price is directly linked to the quality of one's field view, and to make attendance more affordable to families. Attached is the current price structure for ISU men's home football games at Hancock Stadium. What changes will you make to this price plan and with what rationale? Who will receive price discounts to the full price of a game ticket and why?

4. The Wilson Racquet Center is a private operation and has recently remodeled its facility to total 6 racquetball courts and 8 indoor tennis courts. Demand for tennis and racquetball is highest on Mondays, Tuesdays, and Wednesdays between 6:00 and 9:00 a.m., 4:00 and 7:00 p.m., and anytime on a Saturday. Demand for courts is lowest on Sundays and on Friday evenings. All other days and times have moderate demand patterns. Court fees are charged by the hour on top of a base membership fee. Develop a pricing strategy for tennis and racquetball that takes into account the peak periods of demand.

# Fees and Policies

## Membership Options ................................

### Fitness Plus

**Resident**

| Membership Type | Full Price | | |
|---|---|---|---|
| | Initiation | Monthly | Yearly |
| Individual | $150 | $29.00 | $327 |
| Couple | $250 | $44.50 | $502 |
| Family | $350 | $55.00 | $620 |

### Non-Resident

| Membership Type | Full Price | | |
|---|---|---|---|
| | Initiation | Monthly | Yearly |
| Single | $200 | $36.25 | $409 |
| Couple | $300 | $57.00 | $643 |
| Family | $400 | $72.50 | $818 |

- A couple is two living in the same household.
- A family is two adults and children under 21 years living in the same household.
- Youths ages 11-16 on Family Memberships have limited access to the fitness floor and track, and 11-13 year olds must receive orientation and be supervised by an adult.

### Daytime Senior or Junior

Hours: 5:30 a.m. - 6 p.m. — Mon.-Fri.
All day Sat. & Sun. — Courts usage anytime.

**Resident**

| Membership Type | Full Price | | |
|---|---|---|---|
| | Initiation | Monthly | Yearly |
| Individual | $76 | $23.50 | $265 |
| Couple (Sr. Only) | $120 | $37.50 | $423 |

### Non-Resident

| Membership Type | Full Price | | |
|---|---|---|---|
| | Initiation | Monthly | Yearly |
| Individual | $100 | $29.00 | $327 |
| Couple (Sr. Only) | $170 | $46.50 | $525 |

- Senior – ages 65 and older
- Senior Couple – both parties must be 65 or older and living in the same household
- Junior – ages 17-21 years
- Youth – ages 16 and under

### Youth Racquet Sports Membership
Resident - $40    Non-Resident - $60

## Featured Services & Discounts ........................

- Discounted racquet sports lessons & leagues
- Discounted massages
- Free non-prime usage of HB/RB/WB/BB
  Mon-Fri until 4:30 p.m.

- Discounted fitness programs
- Child Care Services
- Free aerobics
- Free Fitness Assessment

## Policies ..................................

1. Please register, with your membership card, at the service desk.
2. The initiation fee is a one -time fee unless membership lapses.
3. Youths under 17 are not allowed in the whirlpool, sauna, steam rooms, or pool. They may use the pool during Family Swim.
4. Monthly dues may be paid through electronic funds transfer from checking or charge accounts.
5. An annual fee may be paid in full and includes 6% discount.
6. Memberships may be upgraded by paying the difference between initiation fees and monthly dues in the existing and upgraded categories.

# SPORT PRICING
## CASE STUDY

The following case study has been included to illustrate the financial considerations in programming a recreational sport event.

Program:  Format - 16 team double elimination softball tournament
Duration - Play begins Friday night, continues
Saturday morning and concludes Sunday afternoon

## Direct Costs

| | | |
|---|---|---:|
| Field Maintenance | $10/game x 31 games = | $ 310 |
| Awards | First place - 12 engraved bats @ $7 = | $ 84 |
| | Second place - 12 specialty softballs @ $4 = | $ 48 |
| Umpires | 2 umpires/game x 31 games = 62 umpire | |
| | games x $20 = | $1240 |
| Balls | 3/game x 31 games =93 balls @ $2 = | $ 186 |
| Promotional Materials | | |
| | Flyers, advertisements, posters, banners | $ 450 |
| Electricity (field lights) 6 night games @ $12 = | | $ 72 |
| Score book | | $    4 |
| Total Direct Costs | | $2394 |

## Indirect Costs

Tournament Coordinator
$25,000 (annual salary) ÷ 52 weeks = $480
12 weeks of tournament work x
10 hours/week = 120 hours or 3/40 hour weeks x $480 =

$1440

## Total Costs                                                                $3834

Tournament Fees/Team to Break Even
16 teams - $240
14 teams - $274

If the event is to break even, team registration fees must be between $240 and $274 depending upon the number of teams entered. Donations or local sponsorships can be obtained to reduce direct costs.

# CHAPTER EIGHT
## Risk Management Applied to Sport

### Introduction

Injuries are often an unfortunate and unwanted side effect of sport and, according to Michener, are so prevalent that each year more injuries are sustained in the United States than casualties in all the American wars combined. This chapter describes the components of a risk management plan to illustrate the measures taken to provide safe, enjoyable sport operations. Changes in traditional sport rules, equipment, and facilities/playing areas used by recreational sport providers to minimize risk are also offered.

### Injuries in Sports

The growth in the provision and participation of sport is directly proportionate to the increase in sport-related injuries. Today, the number of acute sport injuries treated in hospitals is well-known. Four decades ago, sport injuries comprised 1.4% of all injuries seen in an emergency room. During the 1970's, this figure ranged from 5% to 7% and presently approximately 10% of all traumatic injuries are sustained in sports (Renstrom & Kannus, 1988).

The risk of injury to children in sports is an important concern for athletes, parents, coaches, and administrators. There are approximately 20 million children coached by 2.5 million adult volunteers participating in nonschool youth sport programs (Martens, 1980). Many of these volunteer coaches have little or no formal training and tend to rely on their past sports experiences, usually at the high school level, for coaching young children.

A comprehensive study in a midwestern city of 100,000 revealed that younger children had fewer injuries and that the rate of injury increased with age until high school age was attained: 3% of elementary school students, 7% of junior high school students, 11% of high school students sustained severe enough to be treated by a physician (Zaricznyj, Shattuck, & Mast, 1980). There were approximately twice as many injuries in nonorganized sports and in physical education classes as there were in organized sports. The authors felt that 27% of the injuries "could have been avoided had nominal safety precautions been observed."

### Risk Management Plan

A risk management plan specifies written procedures for accident prevention and reduction, and emergency management and is necessary to provide safe sport programs. There are six major stages to a risk management plan: (1) identification of risks and possible emergency situations; (2) provision or requirement of protective devices when appropriate; (3) reduction of such risks through participant and staff education; (4) establishment and enforcement of safety regulations; (5) establishment of emergency procedures; and (6) use of accident/incident report forms.

*1. Identification of Risks and Possible Emergency Situations.*

The first step in a risk management plan is to recognize that certain risks exist. Risks are inherent in virtually every sport. The primary responsibility of a sport programmer is to ensure a safe play environment for participants and to alert them of the potential for injury through participation. This involves regular inspection of playing areas and equipment by various senior agency personnel. The identification of specific risks should not be left to designated agency personnel alone. Every member of the organization should take responsibility for reporting any situation that is viewed as potentially hazardous.

Once risks are identified, the organization must then determine the potential impact or loss due to the hazard (i.e., financial, physical, reputation, etc.) and the appropriate strategy to manage the risks. One option may be to avoid the risk entirely. For example, after careful examination, introducing a white-water kayak race may be too risky physically for the participants and financially for the organizers. The risk is avoided by not staging the event.

Another means of dealing with a risk may be to simply remove it. If the playground basketball hoop is bent, rusty, and jagged, the best answer is to eliminate the problem by having the rim replaced.

Risk reduction is the most common means of managing a hazard. If a sport program is worth retaining, methods must be found to reduce the risks involved while retaining the integrity of the sport. The hazards are usually minimized in one of several ways: (a) use of qualified personnel to conduct the sport; (b) modify the activity and its rules; and (c) ensure that the facilities and equipment are appropriate to the activity and participants.

*2. Provision or Requirement of Protective Devices When Appropriate.*

This may include helmet safety requirements for participation in such sports as football, baseball, fast-pitch softball, hockey, bicycling; eye guards in racquetball; and shin guards in soccer. When selecting sport equipment, care must be taken to ensure it is appropriate for the skill and strength levels of the participants. For example, many youth softball leagues use smaller and lighter bats and balls are larger for ease of hitting and catching.

*3. Reduction of Such Risks Through Participant and Staff Education.*

Prior to many races, event organizers hold a briefing session to outline its various safety requirements. This practice should be followed prior to participation in all sports. Using running racing as an example, race marshall should have received detailed instructions from the race director and be fully aware of emergency procedures. Tiffany (1987) advocates establishing a sport agency group that is responsible for reviewing accidents and injuries, for assisting with inspections and safety training, and for advising on ways to improve and maintain safety procedures.

*4. Establishment and Enforcement of Safety Regulations.*

With the growth in recreational sport participation, accompanied by an increase in sport-related injuries, recreational sport providers have developed, out of necessity, innovative ways of adapting traditional sport rules to ensure the safety of the average citizen participant. For example, the number and severity of leg, ankle, and knee injuries attributed to base sliding in softball and baseball play has led to the establishment of "No-slide" rules in some recreational leagues and tournaments. Equipment manufacturers have developed retractable bases which also slide upon impact, reducing the jarring of body joints and tendons common when contacting traditional bases after a slide. When the baserunner slides into these newer bases with considerable force to cause injury, the base will breakaway from the base anchor. While these new bases may be safer, a recent court decision indicates that a properly installed and maintained anchored base does not necessarily present an unreasonable risk of injury to baserunners (Kozlowski, 1991).

## 5. Establishment of Emergency Procedures.

In the event of an emergency, participants and staff should know the proper procedures to ensure their safety, whether the emergency involves dangerous weather or severe bodily injury to a participant or spectator.

## 6. Use of Accident/Incident Report Forms.

Accident report forms should be used by every sport organization to record all accidents and injuries of a serious or potentially serious nature. Documentation of accidents is necessary for insurance purposes and serves as a tool for managers in evaluating the effectiveness of their risk management plan. The report should include the name and address of the injured party, date and time of accident, and location of the activity that was taken place, nature of the injury, circumstances leading to the injury, name and location of the staff member in charge, treatment given, and names and addresses of two witnesses. Statements by witnesses regarding any *contributory negligence* on the part of the injured party would strengthen the report for the sport organization. Injury report and statement of witness forms should be kept on file for the period specified by state statutory limitations. Some state laws permit litigation to be initiated several years after an accident. Figure 1 contains an example of a sport program accident report form.

## Legal Terms and Concepts

Prior to the discussion of rules of liability for negligent conduct in sports for all, a review of basic legal terms is provided:

1. *Liability* refers to a condition of legal responsibility either by a person or group of persons for their actions as they relate to the safety and well-being of others. When a participant is injured as a result of proved negligence by an agency official, he may be sued to obtain compensation for injury.

2. *Negligence* is an unintentional tort that focuses on an individual's conduct or actions. Negligence occurs when an individual owes a duty to another to protect against unreasonable risk and there is failure to execute reasonable and prudent care toward that person in relation to the situation. Negligence is the primary consideration in any case of liability before damages can be assessed.

Just because an accident occurs and someone is injured does not mean that an agency official was negligent and thus liable. The injury must be clearly linked to some negligent act. The ability of the injured party to sue and recover damages for negligence is based on the idea that one who acts should anticipate the consequences that might involve unreasonable danger to others.

3. *Tort* is the legal term for a civil wrong that infringes on the rights of another. A tortious act is a legal wrong that results in the injury to another individual, group, or damages to property.

4. *Foreseeability* refers to an event or action that could have been prevented by a reasonably prudent person.

5. *Malfeasance* refers to an act of commission *with intent* to hurt, cause harm or otherwise injure another party or his/her property through misconduct or misuse of authority.

6. *Misfeasance* refers to when a person is *actively* involved and liability results from either an act of commission or omission without malicious intent.

7. *Commission*—Injury to second party resulting from incompetence.

8. *Omission*—Individual owes a duty to the participant but does not fulfill that duty.

9. *Nonfeasance* refers to the omission of a lawful act or failure to execute a legal duty when *passively* involved in a situation that results in damage or injury to persons or property.

10. *Attractive Nuisance* is any contrivance that may be alluring to children and potentially dangerous to them.

11. *Defendant*—This term refers to the individual or organization against whom legal action is taken. In a court case involving a sport organization, the defendant may be the manager or any employee of the organization.

12. *Plaintiff*—This is the legal term for the party (individual or group) that initiates legal action against the defendant.

### Factors Required for Proof of Negligence
**Commission of a Tort.** Obviously unless some wrong has been done, there can be no negligence. The tort can include physical, mental, or emotional injury, or property damage. In sport settings, the tort usually involves a case of physical injury to a participant.

**Duty Toward Plaintiff.** For negligence to be proved, it must be clearly shown that the defendant has a duty toward the plaintiff. Sport organizers, coaches, and officials clearly have such a duty toward their participants.

**Breach of Duty.** The person who has a duty must have breached that duty either by an act of omission or commission. The sport organizers who have a duty to players cannot absolve themselves of responsibility by doing nothing when some action on their part is clearly indicated. The person who acts unwisely may be as guilty as the person who acts.

**Proximate Cause of Injury.** The act of commission or omission must be directly linked to the injury by an unbroken chain of events. Only a direct relationship between the imprudent action, or failure to act, and the injury itself can provide grounds for negligence.

## Defense Against Negligence

Courts have identified four basic lines of defense in liability suits involving accidents in recreational sports areas: (1) acts of nature; (2) assumption of risk; (3) contributory negligence; and (4) lack of proximate cause. The following section further defines these terms:

### 1. Acts of Nature

Some injuries that occur are beyond human control and are termed acts of nature. This legal principle has direct implications in sport settings when natural elements such as wind, electrical storms, or earthquakes might lead to a disaster and can clearly be shown to have contributed to unforeseeable injury.

### 2. Assumption of Risk

The principle of this law relates to individuals' voluntary participation in a situation they recognize as having some hazard as a result of their involvement. Regardless of how reasonable the quality of supervision is, injuries may occur as a result of widespread participation in some sports. Waiver forms are particularly useful in alerting participants of potential risks inherent to participation (See Figure 2).

### 3. Contributory Negligence

Contributory negligence occurs most frequently when participants ignore rules regarding an activity, and their subsequent actions is a contributing factor in causing the accident. In such cases, even when there has been an act of omission or commission on the part of a sport provider, the person responsible is absolved of liability.

### 4. Lack of Proximate Cause

For negligence to be present, it must be shown that the behavior of the defendant was directly related to the injury in an unbroken chain of events (proximate cause). When this direct relationship cannot be found, there is no grounds for litigation.

## Waiver Forms

A waiver or release-from-liability form does not release a sport provider from all liability. Courts have taken the stance that the sport provider responsible for a negligent act should be held accountable for the act. Waiver forms may be upheld in courts if the sport provider could not have prevented the incident through reasonable care in the management of the program. In these cases, the courts rule that the participant assumed the risks involved by signing the waiver and thus cannot hold the sport provider responsible for the incident.

Signed releases or waivers of liability in recreational sports may be considered contracts in which the participant agrees to hold the provider of a sporting event free of any fault for acts of negligence. Signed waivers are subject to the same considerations as a contract in a court of law. To avoid the problems of ambiguity, Kozlowski (1991) advises clearly stating in layman's terms, the language of the agreement, and making the waiver conspicuous through the use of larger, bolder and/or color typeface, or other means. The primary objectives are to anticipate the challenges to the signed waiver form that (1) the recreational sports user did not know what he or she was getting into and (2) he or she did not have an adequate opportunity to read and understand the agreement.

Generally, waivers or releases of liability are considered void and against public policy when required by government entities in exchange for the opportunity to participate in a sport. This is particularly true when the governmental service is provided to all citizens, like certain public recreational programs. On the other hand, a recent court decision (*Banfield v. Louis,* 589 So.2d 441) described waiver of liability agreements involving government entities may be valid where the activity at issue involves a sport in which "an infinitely small percentage of the public appear to participate," like triathlons. Explains Kozlowski (1992), "Under such rather limited circumstances, a governmental agency sponsoring and/or promoting an activity which is of not great public interest or a necessary service may receive the benefit of a valid and enforceable waiver agreement."

A consent or waiver form should be comprised of three parts: (1) acknowledgement of the nature of the activity; (2) agreement to follow the rules of the activity; and (3) affirmation of satisfactory physical condition. Figure 2 contains an example of a waiver form used in a community-sponsored running race.

To summarize this section of waivers or release agreements, such contracts against liability for negligence are valid except in those cases where a public interest is involved or where the negligent act falls greatly below the standard established by law for the protection of others against reasonable harm. Mountaineering, scuba diving, sky diving, auto racing, white-water rafting and other high adventures recreational activities have not been found to involve public interest.

## Areas of Potential Negligence In Sport

Recreational sport organizers should become familiar with the most common causes of litigation so that they may take the necessary steps to minimize the possibilities of injury and threat of legal action. This section discusses some of the most common areas of potential negligence in recreational sport settings.

### 1. Inadequate Supervision

Proper ratios of supervisors to participants must be maintained throughout the sport program. Most sport governing bodies and local associations such as Little League, Youth Football Association, and Youth Soccer League have recommended supervision to participant levels or ratios. Playing field supervision and maintenance is equally critical. Employees must be trained to recognize potential hazards in the field. Educational training and workshops on hazard identification must be provided.

## 2. Inappropriate Selection of Activities

Activities should be aimed at meeting the goals and objectives of the participants with their safety as the primary consideration. This is particularly important during sport training. Horror stories abound regarding improper training regimens dictated to students by coaches and trainers. For example, one wrestling coach required some of his athletes to wear rubber sweat suits and run in place in a sauna in hopes to quickly drop a few pounds and "make weight" for a meet. This practice contributed to the athletes' severe dehydration and heat exhaustion.

## 3. Inadequate Control

Measures must be taken to ensure the safety of all sport participants. If a player is intentionally injuring others or fighting, she should be removed from play and warned of punishment for similar actions in the future.

## 4. Transportation

The transportation of participant to and from competition poses a very serious area for litigation. It is imperative that sport program organizers give careful consideration to the implications of transportation available. Chartered commercial vehicles are generally recognized as the most desirable mode of transporting sport participants. The safety record and reputation of the commercial carrier should be thoroughly checked before selection. Organization representatives should expect to see a copy of the business' license to transport persons and its insurance coverage.

## 5. Hazardous Facilities and Equipment

Whenever sport facilities and equipment are unsafe or defective, the organization and those staff members directly involved are vulnerable to legal action if the unsafe equipment results in an accident. This reinforces the importance of regular inspection of facilities and equipment. All defective equipment should immediately be removed. Protective equipment such as helmets, pads, and guards should also be carefully inspected at regular intervals.

## Conclusions

Recreational sport programming is indeed a risky business. Rising public awareness has created a plethora of lawsuits and more of them are reaching the courts. Recreational sport providers should be aware of the basic principles of a liability suit and the means to avoid it. Sport organizations that have established risk management plans have reduced the possibility of liability suits and are able to continue to meet their participants' increasing sport needs. With intelligent planning, administrative support, and an on-going risk management plan, sport programs and services can be improved, expanded, and made safe for all.

## Summary

Recreational sport managers must do everything within their power to minimize the possibility of legal action against the staff and/or organization. A risk management plan specifies written procedures for accident prevention and reduction, and emergency management. This paper outlines the key components of a sport risk management plan.

The first step in a risk management plan is identification of all risks and possible emergency situations inherent to the sport program. Once risks have been identified, decisions must be made whether to retain, avoid, remove or reduce the risks and the means to do so.

The second stage of a risk management plan involves the provision or requirement of protective devices when appropriate. This may include helmet safety requirements for participation in such sports as football, baseball, fast-pitch softball, hockey, bicycling; eye guards in racquetball; and shin guards in soccer.

Participant and staff education is central to stage three of the risk management plan. Employees must be trained to assist with facility and equipment inspections and required to advise on ways to improve and maintain safety procedures.

Establishment and enforcement of safety regulations and emergency procedures are critical components of the next phase of a risk management plan. Recreational sport providers have developed out of necessity, innovative ways of adapting traditional sport rules to ensure the safety of the average citizen participant while maintaining the true integrity of the sport. In the event of an emergency, participants and staff should know the proper procedures to ensure their safety. Such information often is presented to participants in writing and reinforced during a pre-game safety briefing.

Accident report forms constitute the final phase of the risk management plan and should be used by every sport organization to record all accidents and injuries of a serious or potentially serious nature. Documentation of accidents is necessary for insurance purposes and serves as a tool for managers in evaluating the effectiveness of their risk management plan.

The most common areas of potential negligence in recreational sport settings are inadequate supervision; inappropriate selection of activities; inadequate control; transportation; and hazardous facilities and equipment.

There are four factors required for proof of negligence: (1) commission of a tort; (2) duty toward plaintiff; (3) breach of duty; and (4) proximate cause of injury. The tort can include physical, mental, or emotional injury, or property damage. In sport settings, the tort usually involves a case of physical injury to a participant. For negligence to be proved, it must be clearly shown that the defendant has a duty toward the plaintiff. The person who has a duty must have breached that duty either by an act of omission or commission. The sport organizers who have a duty to players cannot absolve themselves of responsibility by doing nothing when some action on their part is clearly indicated. The person who acts unwisely may be as guilty as the person who acts. Only a direct relationship between the imprudent action, or failure to act, and the injury itself can provide grounds for negligence.

Four basic lines of defense in liability suits involving accidents in recreational sports areas include: (1) acts of nature; (2) assumption of risk; (3) contributory negligence; and (4) lack of proximate cause. Waiver or release-from-liability forms have also been found to serve as a defense in such law suits. Acts of nature have direct implications in sport settings when natural elements such as wind, electrical storms, or earthquakes might lead to a disaster and can clearly be shown to have contributed to unforeseeable injury. Assumption of risk relates to individuals' voluntary participation in a situation they recognize as having some hazard as a result of their involvement. Regardless of how reasonable the quality of supervision is, injuries may occur as a result of widespread participation in some sports. Contributory negligence occurs most frequently when participants ignore rules regarding an activity, and their subsequent actions is a contributing factor in causing the accident. For negligence to be present, it must be shown that the behavior of the defendant was directly related to the injury in an unbroken chain of events (proximate cause). When this direct relationship cannot be found, there is no grounds for litigation. Waivers or release agreements are valid contracts except in those cases where a public interest is involved or where the negligent act falls greatly below the standard established by law for the protection of others against reasonable harm.

## References

Kozlowski, J. C. (1988). A common sense view of liability. *Parks and Recreation*, September: 56-59.

Kozlowski, J. C. (1989). Fitness factor in fun run fatality. *Parks and Recreation*, August: 14.

Martens, R. (1980). The uniqueness of the young athlete: Psychological considerations. *American Journal of Sports Medicine*, 8: 382-385.

Mellion, M. B. (1988). Special issues in youth sports. In (Mellion, M. B., Ed.) *Sport Injuries and Athletic Problems*. Philadelphia: Hanley & Befus, Inc.

Michener, J. A. (1976). *Sport in America*. New York: Random House.

Renstrom, P. & Kannus, P. (1988). Prevention of sport injuries. In (Strauss, R. H., Ed.) *Sports Medicine* (2nd ed.). Philadelphia: W. B. Saunders Company.

Tiffany, A. (1987). How to tame the liability monster. *Parks and Recreation*, 22(1): 64-72, 103.

Zaricznyj, B., Shattuck, L. M. & Mast, T. A. (1980). Sports-related injuries in school-aged children. *American Journal of Sports Medicine*, 8: 318-324.

Figure 1

## SPORT PROGRAM ACCIDENT REPORT

PROGRAM_____     DATE_____

LOCATION_____

TIME OF ACCIDENT_____ (a.m.)
(p.m.)

TIME REPORTED_____ (a.m.)
(p.m.)

REPORTED BY
(Supervisor)_____

PERSON(S) INVOLVED:
_____
                        (Name)                                          (Age)
_____
                        (Address)                                       (Phone)
_____
                        (Name)                                          (Age)
_____
                        (Address)                                       (Phone)

WITNESS(ES):
_____
                        (Name)                                          (Age)
_____
                        (Address)                                       (Phone)

WITNESS(ES)
STATEMENT:_____
_____

WITNESS(ES)
SIGNATURE:_____

VICTIM'S SIGNATURE:
_____

SUPERVISOR(S) INVOLVED:
_____

TYPE OF ACCIDENT:

DETAILS OF ACCIDENT AND ACTION TAKEN:
_____
_____

WAS AMBULANCE CALLED? Yes_____ No_____ POLICE? Yes_____ No_____

RECOMMENDATIONS TO SUPERVISOR(S) INVOLVED:
_____
_____

REVIEWED BY:

_____
PROGRAM SUPERVISOR                          DATE

_____
SPORTS & FACILITIES COORD.               DATE

_____
DIRECTOR OF ORGANIZATION               DATE

Figure 2

## RECREATIONAL SPORT WAIVER FORM

_____
**Signature**                                    **Date**

In consideration of your accepting this entry, I, the above signed, intending to be legally bound, hereby, for myself, my heirs, executors and administrators, waive and release any and all rights and claims for damages I may have against the Kenosha Running Club, the counties, cities and villages in which the race is contested, and their affiliates, agents, servants, employees, assigns, successors, and heirs and any other sponsors and their representatives, successors, and assigns for any and all injuries suffered by me in said event.

I attest and verify that that I am physically fit and have sufficiently trained for the completion of this event, recognize that risks of injury accompany such participation and acknowledge that this release is being relied upon by the above persons in permitting me to participate. Further, I hereby grant full permission to any and all of the foregoing to use my name, likeness and voice, as well as any photographs, videotapes, motion pictures, recordings, and any other record of this event in which I may appear for any legitimate purpose including television broadcast of the event, the reuse in any media of this broadcast and in advertising and promotion for such broadcast and reuse.

# CHAPTER NINE
## Running Race Management

### Introduction

Running is one of the most popular forms of physical exercise in the United States. The National Running Data Center (NRDC) reports that 30 million Americans run at least twice per week, 14 percent of the total population (1987). Of the 30 million runners in the United States, The Athletic Congress (TAC) estimated that 1.1 million ran in organized races in 1986. TAC further revealed that 5,342 prominent races were conducted during the same year. TAC statisticians believe this figure represents only one-half of all races actually held in the United States. The NRDC projects that the number of organized running races will increase at a rate of 5 percent annually. A majority of these races are organized by private businesses (e.g., sporting goods stores) and nonprofit organizations (e.g., running clubs). It is unknown what percentage of the total number of organized running races are conducted by municipal park and recreation departments. It is speculated that races organized by local park and recreation departments are small in scale and thus not included in TAC statistical data of race organizers. However, a department's conservative recreation philosophy, limited operational budget, and lack of staff expertise and resources may possibly explain why municipalities infrequently organize running races.

The effects of running on personal fitness have been well documented (ACSM, 1992). There are also quantifiable economic benefits that a community may receive as a result of conducting a running race. An analysis of the economic impact of the San Francisco Marathon to the city found that $6.6 million was directly spent by participants and spectators in hotels, restaurants and shops during the race weekend. It was also determined that the city collected over $250,000 in hotel/motel tax receipts (Wagner, 1984). By showing city officials the economic benefits of hosting a running race through detailed economic impact studies, continued local government and business support for the event may be achieved.

There are significant, but non-quantifiable benefits which result from holding a running race which will accrue to the local area over time. Intangible and indirect benefits such as recognition, civic pride, media coverage and the chance to show off the community at its best have a positive effect on the city or town's economic environment which can only be measured in the long term, if at all.

There has been a considerable amount of published material dealing with the sport of running. The majority of the literature pertains to the sport itself. Unfortunately, little literature or research has been devoted to running race organization, particularly by municipal park and recreation departments. Organizing a running event requires special planning in several program areas like safety, registration, timing/scoring and logistics. The purpose of this chapter is to provide running race managers with a guide that may assist them in organizing a running race that is safe and enjoyable for all concerned.

## Purpose of the Race

What is the reason for the race's existence? The purpose of the race will dictate the nature of its programming elements. Is the race to determine the swiftest of the swift, to provide a morning of physical exercise in a social setting, or both? A *fun run* is considered a non-competitive, organized running activity of any distance that is free of charge to its participants. In contrast, a running *race* is an organized, competitive running contest featuring paid participant registration and timing elements, covering a distance of one mile or greater.

Frequently, races are held in conjunction with a larger extravaganza in a community such as a festival, anniversary celebration, or parade. The "Firecracker Five" a five mile race in Kenosha, Wisconsin serves to "warm-up" the crowd for the city's Fourth of July parade. What distance should the event be? Remember, most "weekend warriors" will have difficulty running more than 10K. Consider offering two distances for participants to choose to run (e.g., 10K and 5K). Below are examples of various running race themes:

*Jingle Bells Jog* - (December) Participants are given tiny bells to wear on their shoes during the race.

*Shirt-Off-Your Back Run* - Entry fee is a t-shirt from another race in good condition. Racers select a t-shirt from the pile in order of finish.

*Turkey Trot* - Turkeys are awarded to the race winners; chickens and game hens to the runner-ups.

*Valentine's Day Run* - Racers register as a couple. Winners are determined by combined time. A romantic dinner for two is first prize; flowers and chocolates are door prizes.

*Mother's Day Dash* - Special mom and child categories - their combined times determine the winner.

*Halloween Howl* - Costumed race with trick-or-treat aid stations. Costume contest and dance following the race.

*April Fool's Day Five* - A phony finish line is staged after the actual finish line. Runners may be "fooled" as to which is the real finish line.

## Getting Started

Table 1 is a partial list of running race planning considerations and should convince the race director not to attempt to organize the event alone. Form an event planning committee comprised of energetic, hard working, knowledgeable people. Recruit track and cross-country coaches and enthusiasts, sporting goods retailers or running club leaders as members.

Also included on the race central planning committee should be representatives from the police, public works and fire departments. Assign each to a specific area of responsibility under the following major headings: registration, sponsorship, publicity, logistics, safety, timing and scoring, awards, and refreshments. Plan early and thoroughly; preparations for a large-scale race may require year-round planning. Prepare a checklist with planning tasks and required completion dates to assist your committee.

TABLE 1

### Running Race Considerations

_____ Race Committee Formed
_____ Budget Plan
_____ Insurance Coverage
_____ Route Approval

_____ Volunteer Recruitment/Training
      _____ Determine human resource requirements

_____ Promotional Plan
    Flyers        Posters        Banners Advertisements
    Billboards    Direct mail          Publicity        Incentives

_____ Timing/Scoring System
_____ Race categories
_____ Awards

_____ Risk Management Plan
      _____ Secure Medical/Rescue Service
      _____ Security Arrangements
      _____ Emergency Medical Procedures

_____ Determine Pre- and Post-Race Activities
_____ Conduct Cost-Benefit Analysis
_____ Sponsorship Plan and Implementation
_____ Pre-race Briefing

_____ Registration System
      _____ Pre-Race Registration
          _____ Method of Payment      _____ Participant Fee Discounts
_____ Contingency Plan
      _____ What will be done in the event of inclement weather?
      Postpone Race    Shorten Race Length    Add Race Aid Stations
_____ Evaluation
      _____ Racer satisfaction
      _____ Post-Race Committee Meeting

# FIGURE 1

## Running Race Flow Chart

| Task | J | F | MR | A | Month MY | JN | JL |
|---|---|---|---|---|---|---|---|
| Race Committee | | | | | | | |
|   Race Design | 9 | | | | | | |
|   Race Route Approval | | 12 | | | | | |
| Budget Plan | | | 3 | | | | |
| Sponsorship Solicitation | | 18 | | | | | |
| Promotional Plan | | | | 22 | | | |
| Timing/Scoring System | | | | | 8 | | |
|   Race categories | | | | | 8 | | |
|   Awards | | | | | | | 27 |
| Risk Management Plan | | | | | | | |
|   Secure Medical/Rescue Service | | 10 | | | | | |
|   Security Arrangements | | | | 15 | | | |
|   Emergency Medical Procedures | | | | | 11 | | |
| Volunteer Recruitment | | | | | 25 | | |
| Implementation | | | | | | | 4 |
| Evaluation | | | | | | | |
|   Cost-Benefit Analysis | | | | | | | 20 |

Flow charts have been mentioned in recreation program planning literature as a key tool in managing recreation programs (Rossman, 1990; Farrell & Lundegren, 1987). This technique identifies and prioritizes specific tasks that must be completed to successfully conduct the program. A time line is often developed with the flow chart indicating what tasks are to be done, when they will be done, how long the task will take to complete, and who will be responsible for doing the task. Below is an example of a flow chart for a community running race with the numbers underneath the months indicating the day in which the task was completed.

Schedule a date that avoids direct competition with other established area races and is convenient with Mother Nature. For example, it would be inappropriate to organize a race in Milwaukee on the same weekend as Al's Run, which annually features over 20,000 racers primarily from the midwest. A race start time of 1:00 p.m. in July is equally ill-advised. For most areas of the country the mean temperature during this time of day and year is between 80 - 95° F, temperatures too warm for most racers.

# Safety

Your first responsibility and priority as race director should be to ensure the safety of all who attend the event - racers, spectators, volunteers and staff. Chapter Eight provides a thorough discussion of risk management procedures that should be applied to running race management. The following list gives the reader an indication of the number of safety considerations involved in a running race:

1. Race headquarters should be located near the finish line and include a staffed, first-aid station and communication equipment.

2. Secure arrangements with the local hospital and fire department rescue squad to provide race-site care equipment. Volunteer medical assistance may be obtained through local chapters of national agencies such as the American Heart Association, American Red Cross, and American Lung Association.

3. One safety marshall should be stationed at every kilometer point along the race course.

4. Race marshalls and aid station personnel should have current First Aid and CPR certifications.

5. Provide course marshalls with a walkie-talkie and emergency first-aid supplies.

6. Aid stations with water and/or carbohydrate sports drinks should be positioned on the course every 2 kilometers and include safety marshalls with medical equipment and supplies.

7. Races greater than 10K in distance should include portable toilets and at each aid station.

8. Special one-day liability insurance may be required by your local government for the event. Premium costs may range from $500 to $2,500 depending on the nature of the activity.

9. Shorten or postpone the race in the event of inclement weather (i.e., high humidity and temperature, lightning, hail, etc.).

10. Every racer must sign the race waiver form and be alerted of the inherent risks to racing. Racers under 18 years must have a parent or guardian sign the waiver form.

11. Provide a motorized escort to lead racers through the course. An escort service should also follow the last racers to ensure their safety or to aid racers along the course.

12. Conduct a pre-race briefing which outlines the safety measures and race course features.

13. No bicycles, rollerblades, roller skates, skateboards, or rollerskis permitted on the course.

14. Arrange with local police to "control" intersections, thereby insuring the runners right-of-way.

## Registration

The popularity of running races has produced growing pains for several major road races. In 1981, New York City Parks Commissioner, Gordon Davis, imposed a 16,000 runner limit on the New York City Marathon. As a result, 44,000 race applications were returned after the entry limit was met. The 1984 Grandma's Marathon held in Duluth, Minnesota, received its 20,000 entry limit in the first five days of race registration.

Some races, such as the Cherry Blossom 10-miler in Washington, D. C., have conducted entry lotteries to select participants. The 1983 Bay to Breakers 12 kilometer race, located in San Francisco, paid no attention to entry limits. A field of 60,000 registered runners and an estimated 20,000 unofficial runners participated. It was reported that it took the final starter 25 minutes to reach the designated starting line (RRM, 1983).

Take steps to make it as easy as possible for the runners to enroll in the race. Requiring pre-race day registration to participate in an race makes things less hectic on race day, but it also prevents those spontaneous recreators who decide that morning to run in the race from doing so. As many as 55 percent of the total number of runners can be gained through race-day registration. It is common practice, however, to offer a reduced fee to those persons registering two weeks before the event (e.g., $8 pre-race, $12 race-day). If offering race day registration, be prepared for a rush of racers with several persons designated to facilitate this process. Some races give participants who register in advance of the race receive T-Shirts displaying the caption, "In training for the --- Race." This method is an excellent method of encouraging early registration and also serves as a form of race promotion.

Event directors, in attempt to expand the pool of runners, often provide opportunities for both the competitive and non-competitive runner during the same running event (e.g., 10 K race and 5 K fun run/walk). Offering team relay categories is another method employed to attract more race participants.

Race registration forms should provide participants with the following information:

    1. Race date, time, sponsor(s) location and directions to race start
    2. Route and description of terrain, grade
    3. Registration deadline, fee, t-shirts
    4. Race categories, awards

5. Aid stations, mile split times, refreshments
6. Restrictions
7. Contact for additional information
8. Liability waiver

Figures 2, 3, 4 contain examples of running race registration forms.

## Logistical Arrangements

The challenges facing running race logistical coordinators have been likened to those of an army general during battle. When determining the race course and location, consider whether the sites have suitable terrain for running, adequate parking for the estimated number of racers/spectators, electricity, running water, and is accessible to special populations. Local parks, athletic fields and community centers are common race sites because they have these features. Arrange with local police to provide security and traffic control at intersections where high automobile volume may be a safety hazard. Notify law enforcement officials and neighboring businesses of the potential traffic and parking problems that may result from the number of runners arriving to the race area by automobile. Portable toilets are needed if an indoor facility is not available that cannot accommodate the sanitation needs of the event attendees. It's a dirty job but somebody has to plan for it.

Race courses are designed in one of three directions: out-and-back, circuit, or direct route. An out-and-back race course features the same start and finish location. As the name implies, participants race to the designated half-way point and return along the same route. Circuit races require participants to complete two or more laps on the same course. For example, an event featuring 5K and 10K races on a 5K cross-country course would simply require 10K participants to run two laps. The direct route race design starts at one location and finishes at another. A drawback of the direct route design is that racers must be find transportation either back or to the starting area. Most races using this course design provide complimentary transportation for the racers. An advantage of this course design is its minimal disruption to vehicular traffic. Figures 5 and 6 contain examples of road race routes.

Kenosha News

Kenosha Hospital & Medical Center

## ★★★★★★FIRECRACKER 5★★★★★★

The annual Firecracker 5 offers participants their choice of a 5 kilometer run or a 1.2 mile walk/run in front of thousands of spectators along the Kenosha County Veterans Civic Parade route. The Firecracker 5 is part of Star Spangled Kenosha Days, June 26-July 5.

### Contributors
AMTA (American Massage Therapy Association), Don Gill Bicycle Shop, Kenosha Twins, Nike, Pepsi Cola, Pizza Hut, Ski and Sport Chalet, Southport Rigging and Super Sports Footwear, etc.

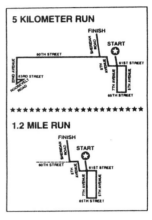

**5 KILOMETER RUN**

★★★★★★★★★★★★★★★★★★★★★★★

**1.2 MILE RUN**

---

**Firecracker 5 Entry Form**

*Please print using a ball point pen*

Event: ☐ 5K run ☐ 1.2 mile run ☐ 1.2 mile walk

Last name                    First name

Address

City                    State    Zip

Wheelchair    Sex    Age on 7/5/92    Date of Birth
☐            ☐                        

Phone number
☐☐☐ / ☐☐☐ - ☐☐☐☐

**Team entry (5K only):** ☐ Corporate ☐ Novice ☐ Club
Team name

*Team members should submit entries in one envelope*

**Entry fee:** Pre-registration $9.00 (Deadline Sat. July 4, 1992)
Race day $11.00 (Register by 1:00 p.m.)
Senior Citizens (60 and over) $7.00
Youth (15 and under) $7.00

**Mail entries to:** Firecracker 5, Kenosha Youth Foundation
720 59th Place Kenosha, Wisconsin 53140

**T-shirt:** Adult ☐ S ☐ M ☐ L ☐ XL  Youth: ☐ M

In consideration of the foregoing, I for myself, my heirs, executors, and administrators, waive and release any and all rights and claims for damages I may have against the Kenosha Youth Foundation, the City of Kenosha, Kenosha Hospital and Medical Center, the Kenosha News and any and all participating sponsors and supports for all claims of damages, demands, actions, whatsoever in any manner as a result of participating in the Firecracker 5. I attest and verify that I am physically fit and have sufficiently trained for the completion of this event and my physical condition has been verified by a licensed medical doctor. Further, I hereby grant full permission to any and all of the foregoing to use my likeness for any purpose whatsoever.

Signature of parent (if under 18)
_____

Signature _____

# Race Information

### Race Date
Sunday, July 5, 1992
### Distances
A 5 kilometer road race and a 1.2 mile fun run/walk
### Starting Times
1.2 mile fun run/walk - 1:00 p.m.
5 kilometer road race - 1:15 p.m.
### Race Site
Both events will begin at the corner of 7th Avenue and 60th Street and finish on Sheridan Road in front of the parade reviewing stand.
### Entry Fees
Entry fees are $9 if registered before July 5. Same day registration is $11 and will be accepted until 1:00 p.m. Pre-registration and race day fee for youths (15 and under) and senior citizens (60 and over) is $7. Make checks payable to : FIRECRACKER 5.
### Team Competition
The FIRECRACKER 5 will feature team competition for the 5 kilometer event. There will be three divisions: **Corporate, Competitive Club and Novice Teams.** Each team must consist of at least four runners. The winning teams are determined by the combined times of the first four team finishers.
### Age Groups
1.2 Mile Run: 5-6, 7-8, 9-10, 11-12, 13-14, 15-16, 17-19, 20-24, 25-29, 30-34, 35-39, 40-44, 45-49, 50-54, 55-59, 60 and over.
5K Run: 14 and under, 15-19, 20-24, 25-29, 30-34, 35-39, 40-44, 45-49, 50-54, 55-59, 60 and over.
### Awards
Ribbons will be presented to the top three finishers for each age group in the 1.2 mile run. Awards will be given to the first three finishers in each age division and the wheelchair division of the 5 K run. Plaques will be given to the first place division winners. Medals will be awarded to the second and third place finishers.

### Packet Pick Up
Pre-registered entrants can pick up their race packets starting June 29 at the KYF Main Desk or after 11:00 a.m., July 5 in the KYF Multi-Purpose Room.
**T-shirts will be given to the first 500 registered entrants.**
### Refreshments
Post-race refreshments provided by Pepsi Cola General Bottlers, Inc. of Kenosha and Racine. Water will also be available.
### Waterstops and First Aid
Waterstops will be along the course. Emergency aid will be provided by the Scout Leaders Rescue Squad during the race and at the finish.
### Timing
Computerized timing performed by C.A.R.R. S.
**No event times will be registered for walkers.**
### Results
Race results will be tabulated by computerized timing. Overall results will be printed in the Kenosha News July 6.
### Post-Race Activities
Awards will be presented during the post-race festivities in the Civic Center.
All participants are eligible to win valuable door prizes during the awards ceremony. Each registered runner and walker are automatically entered.
Following the race, members of the American Massage Therapy Association will be on hand to provide post-race sport massages. This 15-minute massage will help relieve muscular soreness and assist in the removal of lactic acid from the muscles.
Stay after the event and watch one of the midwest's best parades. The Kenosha County Veterans Civic Parade follows the FIRECRACKER 5.
### Information
24-hour phone information is available. Telephone the Kenosha Youth Foundation at (414) 654-2104.

Firecracker 5
Kenosha Youth Foundation
720 59th Place
Kenosha, Wisconsin 53140

145

**Country Companies**
**Town of Normal • WJBC**

# Fall Fitness Classic

*Town of Normal • Country Companies • WJBC*
*Sunday, October 4th • 1:00 p.m.*
*At Maxwell Park, Normal*

**Fall Fitness Classic**

Sanctioned and Certified by Illinois TAC

## Services to Runners and Walkers

- **POST-RACE MEAL**
- Water Stops
- First-aid Stations
- Restrooms
- Electronic Clock at finish
- Mile splits for 10-Mile Race at 1-2-3-5-6.2-8
- Mile splits for 5K Race and 5K Fitness Walk
- Refreshments at finish lines
- Plenty of free parking
- Computerized time printouts will be mailed to 10-Mile and 5K Race Participants
- Live Entertainment

## For more Information

Contact the Town of Normal Parks and Recreation Department at (309) 454-9540.

The Town of Normal, the Country Companies insurance group and WJBC AM-1230 are once again sponsoring the annual Fall Fitness Classic. The Fall Fitness Classic includes 10-Mile and 5K Races, and a 5K Fitness Walk. The races and walk are meant to encourage people to enjoy the benefits of healthy physical activity.

## Registration

Save time and money by preregistering and mailing the attached form by September 25, 1992. All registrants will receive a post-race meal. Race day registration is 10:00 a.m. to 12:30 p.m. at Maxwell Park.

## Entry Fees (non-refundable)

Pre-registration entry fees are good through September 25, 1992. There are three entry fees: $10 for individual without a t-shirt; $15 for individual with a commemorative long-sleeved T-shirt; and $20 for a family of three or more plus $7 per commemorative long-sleeved t-shirt.

Late registration entry fees are: $15 for individual without a t-shirt; $20 for individual with a commemorative long-sleeved T-shirt; and $25 for family entry fee for families of three or more without t-shirts.

Employees of the Town of Normal, WJBC/WBNQ Radio, the Country Companies, Illinois Agricultural Association and Growmark receive a $2 discount on the pre-registration entry fee.

## Courses/Times

All courses begin at Maxwell Park on Parkside Road and follow well-marked, patrolled courses through city and county roads back to Maxwell Park. (See map on reverse side for directions to Maxwell Park.) The 10-mile race course is officially certified by The Athletic Congress (TAC). All events begin at 1:00 p.m.

Race awards will be presented to the top female and male finisher in the 10-Mile and 5K races. In addition,

awards will be presented to the top three male and female finishers in each of the following age categories for both races:

| 18 and under | 30-34 | 45-49 |
| 19-24 | 35-39 | 50-59 |
| 25-29 | 40-44 | 60 and over |

## 5K Fitness Walk

As part of an ongoing effort to promote the benefits of a healthy lifestyle we offer a 5K Fitness Walk. Walkers will follow a separate 5K route than the runners. Although not a competitive event, participants may walk or race/walk at any rate they choose. All registered walkers will be eligible for merchandise awards. Bring a friend - or your entire family - and enjoy a fun, healthy afternoon.

## Award Decisions

All awards will be presented immediately following the race. All decisions of race officials are final.

## Merchandise

All participants are eligible for merchandise awards. Merchandise awards (approximately 100) will be made by random selection.

Commemorative, long-sleeve T-shirts will be on sale for $10.

## Post-Race Meal

All participants may enjoy the free post-race meal. The meal includes: Grilled Butterfly Pork Chops, fruit salad, pasta salad and drinks.

## Special Event

BroMenn HealthCare will provide fitness testing and health information for participants and race fans alike.

## Special Thanks

Special thanks go to the McLean County Road Runners and the Lake Run Club for cosponsoring this event, helping with volunteers and offering their racing expertise.

---

Name_____ Phone_____

Address_____

City_____ State____ Zip_____

☐ Male  ☐ Female   Age_____ (as of October 4)

**Special Information**
☐ IAA/Country Companies/Growmark Employee/Agent
☐ Town of Normal Employee   ☐ WJBC Employee

**Event:** (circle only one) 10-Mile Run   5K Run   5K Walk

**Entry Fee:** (circle only one)   $10 (individual)
                                    $15 (individual with shirt)

$20 (family of 3 or more) + 7 x ____ (number of shirts) = _____

**Shirt size:**   S___ M___ L___ XL___ XXL___

$2 discount to employees of Country Companies, IAA, Growmark, Town of Normal and WJBC/WBNQ Radio. (Make checks payable to Town of Normal)

**Mail to:**  Fall Fitness Classic
              Town of Normal
              P.O. Box 589
              Normal, IL 61761

In consideration of this entry being accepted, I for myself, my executors, administrators and assignees, do hereby waive, release and discharge all rights and claims for damages against the Town of Normal, each of the Country Companies, Twin Cities Broadcasting, and all other sponsors, including their directors, officers and employees, for any injury, sickness or loss to me arising out of or sustained in connection with my participation in the 1992 Town of Normal/Country Companies/WJBC Fall Fitness Classic. Further, I assume all risks associated with running and/or walking in this event including but not limited to, falls, contact with other participants, the effects of weather (including high heat and/or humidity), traffic and conditions of the road, all such risks being known and appreciated by me.

I further attest that I know running and/or walking a road race is a potentially hazardous activity and that I am in good health and have sufficiently trained for the competition of this event. I hereby grant permission to the Town of Normal, the Country Companies group, and Twin Cities Broadcasting to use my name and any photographs, motion pictures, recordings, or any other record of this event for any purpose without obligations.

Signature of entrant_____ Date_____

Signature _____ Date_____
                    (parent or guardian if under 18)

*List your 1992 TAC number and deduct $1 from your entry fee. TAC #_____

**SIG TAU'S BIATHLON '92**

Saturday, April 25, 1992
Illinois State University
2m run - 12m bike - 2m run

Gatorade THIRST QUENCHER

**PowerBar**
Fuel for Optimum Performance

## YOU ARE INVITED TO THE SIGMA TAU GAMMA BIATHLON !

### PURPOSE

The Sigma Tau Gamma Biathlon is the premier event of its kind in the Bloomington-Normal area and this year is our 8th anniversary. More than 200 people come out annually to compete and join in the fun for a good cause-the American Red Cross and D.A.R.E. (Drugs Awareness, Resistance, and Education).

### COURSE

Fast, challenging Biathlon for serious competitors and/or novice athletes. Start/Finish/Transition located just north of Redbird Arena. A 2 mile run through the residential west end of Normal to transition area. Bike 12 miles through rural McLean County returning to the transition area on to the final 2 mile run through the scenic ISU campus finishing in front of Redbird Arena's north entrance. Aid stations with water, fruit, and energy replacement drink/bars at transition area.

### GIFT ITEMS

Each entrant will receive a Biathlon T-shirt and free entry to the post race celebration. REGISTER BY APRIL 10 AND RECEIVE A COMMEMORATIVE BIATHLON WATERBOTTLE

### ENTRY FEE

$20 per entry. Applications must be delivered to Sigma Tau Gamma NO LATER THAN April 10, 1992. Applications received after that date will be subject to a $7 late fee.

### START TIMES

EARLY ARRIVAL IS ENCOURAGED. THE RACE BEGINS AT 9AM SHARP!

| | |
|---|---|
| 7:00 am | Race day registration and check-in begin. |
| 8:00 am | Late registration ends. |
| 8:30 am | Check-in ends/warm up |
| **9:00 am** | **RACE STARTS** |
| 11:00 am | Awards presentation |
| T.B.A. | Post-race celebration |

### AGE BRACKETS

Awards will go to the top three male and female finishers in each of the following age groups:
18-24     25-34     35+
Product awards given as bonus.

### HOTEL ACCOMMODATIONS

If you are coming in from out of town, special room rates are available at the Holiday Inn-Normal North. (8 Traders Circle). To receive the special rate, call 1-800-HOLIDAY. Identify yourself as a Sig Tau Biathlon Participant in Normal, IL and give the 3-letter code "STG". Reservations must be made by April 10, 1992.

For more ΣΤΓ Biathlon info call:
**(309) 888-4855**   Director
or **454-2496**   Chapter House

*Helmet required
on bike segment

**Coors LIGHT**

DOMINO'S PIZZA

VITESSE
**Cycle Shop**

B limpie

Holiday Inn
Bloomington Normal North

**DJ EXPRESS**
PROFESSIONAL MUSIC PRODUCTIONS

VIDEO NUTZ

✂ - - - - - - - - - - - - - - - - - - - - - - - - -

**ENTRY FORM (Please print)**

Make checks payable and mail to:   **SIGMA TAU GAMMA**   711 Kingsley Ct. #3, Normal, IL 61761

NAME_____(first)   _____(last)

SEX ___(M) ___(F)   AGE____(race day)   PHONE_____-_____-_____

SCHOOL ADDRESS_____   CITY_____   STATE___ZIP_____

PERMANENT ADDRESS_____   CITY_____   STATE___ZIP_____

EMERGENCY CONTACT_____ PHONE_____-_____-_____

**WAIVER OF LIABILITY**
In consideration of acceptance of this application, for myself, heirs, executors, administrators, guardians and assigns, I waive and release from all liability for and all claims of damages arising as a result of injury to my person or property, including travel to and from the event, due to my participation in the Sigma Tau Gamma Biathlon on April 25, 1992, any and all organizations, sponsors and individuals involved in any respect with said event. I UNDERSTAND THAT I AM REQUIRED TO WEAR A **HELMET** on the entire bike segment of said event. I have read and understand and agree to the above waiver and release.

Participant's signature_____ Date_____

YOUR AWARD BRACKET: (circle one)

| | | | |
|---|---|---|---|
| Male | 18-24 | 25-34 | 35+ |
| Female | 18-24 | 25-34 | 35+ |

**FEES:**

| | | |
|---|---|---|
| Individual entry | $20 | $_____ |
| After 4/10 add | $7 | _____ |
| Extra T-shirts | $8 | _____ |
| Extra waterbottles | $3 | _____ |
| Additional donation- American Red Cross/D.A.R.E | | _____ |
| TOTAL non-refundable | | $_____ |

## Financial Considerations

Race budgets have surpassed the $1 million dollar mark in the New York City, Boston and Chicago Marathons. The average cost expended by race organizers is as high as $52 per runner. In its *Race Director's Handbook*, RRCA (1982) identified five items of considerable expense in race organization: printing, advertising, awards, refreshments and clerical-related services. Racer registration fees are typically used to offset a portion or the total operating expenditures. The proportion of racer registration fees used to cover race expenses is dependent upon the type of organization producing the race (i.e., park district, fitness center, YMCA) and its purpose for holding the event, the number of racers participating, and the total operating expenditures.

## Sponsorship

Securing contributions and donations from the business community can greatly reduce the event's total expenditures. Sponsorship may take the form of cash, merchandise, and/or administrative services. Although national sponsors such as Nike, Miller, and Budweiser Brewing companies, Avon, and Pepsi provide substantial support for a number of races throughout the country, the vast majority of events are sponsored by local businesses or groups (RRM, 1983). This is logical since the most immediate promotional impact for a local company takes place in the locality in which the race is held. Also, there are far more local than national businesses. In a 1983 survey of 100 races conducted by Road Race Management, primary sponsors (largest monetary contributors) were found to be banks, shoe companies, municipalities, health organizations, beverage companies and media stations.

Businesses may be willing to provide refreshments, awards, t-shirts, volunteers, start/finish banners, posters, prizes, technical assistance, or money in exchange for promotional considerations. For sponsors to continue their race support, they must derive over the long term, "...a return of exposure, product or service advertisement, or goodwill." Tinsley states that these three reasons must, in the end, result in sales to generate profit for the sponsor, or a more effective promotional campaign will be sought. Seek out soft drink distributors, banks, grocers, hospitals, convenient stores, eateries, hospitals and hotels/motels. Enlist the assistance of the local chamber of commerce. For larger scale races, contact sporting goods manufacturers (i.e., Brooks, Nike, Converse, etc.) or food producers (i.e, Dannon, Sargento Cheese, Hormel, etc.). Arrangements with these national/regional businesses may need to be made as much as two years in advance of the event's scheduled date. A complete discussion on sport sponsorship may be found in Chapter 9.

## Publicity

A running race is one of the most colorful recreation activities you'll ever see. Imagine hundreds of runners dressed in wild neon-colored nylon dashing through town. What a photo opportunity! Include a costume contest if you want to liven things up even more. Place photos of last year's event in this year's promotional materials. Write feature articles and news releases on the event and submit them to local media sources. Better yet, seek sponsorship with a local news media agency (i.e., newspaper, radio or television station). Obtain mailing lists of runners who participated in other races from organizers and mail your registration forms directly to these individuals and to various running clubs in the area.

## Timing/Scoring

Racers request two things from a race - that the course be the length advertised (if you call it 10K - make sure its 10K, not 5.9 miles) and that their finish time is accurate. Technology available for race management has advanced considerably - some races use electronic bar codes similar to the system used in many grocery stores, to process race results. If available, utilize a chronomix which immediately provides a finisher's time and place on a ticker-tape print out. A large digital race clock positioned at the finish line is also a nice feature. High school track or cross country running coaches or local running clubs may have these gadgets and allow you to borrow them.

For scoring purposes, racers are typically categorized by age and gender. The following is an example of an age group division for a community 10K running race: 9 years and under; 10-14; 15-19; 20-24; 25-29; 30-34; 35-39; 40-44; 45-49; 50-54; 55-59; 60 and above. Depending upon the past or estimated participation in the race, the race organizer may want to combine or add more age categories.

In many races, awards are given to only the top finishers. Consider enlarging the number of winners your event recognizes by creating unique race categories. To encourage family participation, team categories may include parent and child or spouse divisions. Winners of the team competition are determined by the shortest combined time. Cross-country races organized by the University of Wisconsin-Parkside Athletic Department feature participant age and weight divisions. Some races award the racer who most accurately predicts her/his finish time. Costume contests are often included as a side-event in many Halloween races.

To better identify racers in their respective age categories and gender divisions, utilize a color-coded race numbering system. Numbered race bibs often have a peel-off section where racer information (name, age, gender) is placed. As the racers finish, simply remove the information sticker,write the finisher's time on it, and place the sticker on the corresponding age/gender division results poster. Utilize a manual back-up timing/scoring system with stop watches and place cards. It's better to be safe than sorry.

The Athletic Congress (TAC) has recently developed an unique scoring system gaining popularity with race organizers based on finish times collected from numerous races over the years. All racers are given a starting time handicap determined by TACSTATS/USA standards for age and gender. See the chart below:

The advantage to the handicap system is that all racers have the chance to cross the finish line first regardless of age or gender. The system employs a race start handicap in which racers are assigned a start time based on age and gender. Male racers age 73 and above would start the race with an 8.5 minute advantage over males age 24 or 25 years for a 5 kilometer race.

### Prizes/Awards

Everyone likes to come away from a running event with something to remember it by. Most races offer colorful t-shirts to all or most of its participants just for registering. Place the race name and logo on the gift and it will serve as a form of publicity for next year's event. Some events offer pins or ribbons to all finishers.

Medals and plaques for category winners can be inexpensive and convenient to obtain, but unique awards can make the race truly special. Consider commissioning a local artist to create small sculptures, pottery, or prints as top prizes. Door prize drawings for the fabulous prizes your sponsors have donated may allow others to win as well. Running accessories such as shoes, socks, gloves, shorts, sweatsuits, watches and hats are typical door prizes. Winners are selected at random by their race identification numbers.

### Refreshments

This race element is not a necessity but it is a nice amenity. Complementary refreshments like oranges, yogurt, cookies, bananas, juice, carbohydrate replacement drinks, and/or soft drinks are greatly appreciated by the runners after the race. A sponsoring grocer may be willing to provide these goodies. Eating and drinking places will often sponsor a race and realize a substantial return on investment in post-race food and beverage sales. The post event refreshment period also promotes socialization among the participants and may keep them occupied while final race results are being tabulated.

### Volunteers

Large numbers of human resources are needed to conduct a successful race, regardless of participant size. A small 5K running race (80 participants) may require up to 40 volunteers. The 1986 New York City and Chicago Marathons each require over 4,000 volunteers. To further illustrate the importance volunteers to the success of a race, a survey of now-defunct races in Wisconsin revealed lack of volunteer support as the major cause of cancellation (Thompson, 1984).

The use of volunteers also contributes to the financial success of the race. By securing volunteer services of local police officers to control traffic, and fire department personnel for emergency medical service, a city race may save hundreds of dollars. The 1981 San Francisco Marathon paid the City of San Francisco $30,000 for police services during the race. LeBow (1983) stresses the importance of municipal approval and co-sponsorship of running races in an effort to keep operational costs down.

By showing city officials the economic benefits a race can offer through detailed economic impact studies, approval and assistance may be granted. 'Where can I find that many people to help out?' you ask. Recruit volunteers from local civic service organizations like the Women's Club, Jaycees, Kiwanis, scout troops, church groups. If you must, call in personal debts or favors owed to you from friends and family and have them assist during the event.

## Evaluation

Evaluation is often the most neglected aspect of recreation sports programming. However, thorough written evaluations and final race reports may offer a wealth of information in planning next year's race and therefore should not be overlooked. It is recommended that a variety of evaluation methods be employed. Consider implementing a post-race survey of participants through exit interviews, mail evaluation forms or both. An example of a race evaluation survey is appended to this chapter.

The economic impact of a running race may be derived from detailed nonresident participant expenditure surveys and useful in securing sponsorship next year from local businesses. Market information such as the community where the racer is from, how racers heard about the race, and racer demographic information may also be determined through this evaluation technique (See Chapter 7 for a thorough discussion of economic impact assessment procedures). While seeking quantitative information such as attendance, advertising effectiveness, and visitor expenditures, the race evaluator should also attempt to measure qualitative objectives like participant satisfaction and enjoyment. For example, using a Likert scale (1 = excellent, 5 = poor), ask racers questions like "How would you rate the following race components...Timing/Scoring, Registration, Food/Beverages, Safety?"

Video taping the race has been found to be a valuable evaluation tool. In addition to providing a visual reference of the race's various components, it will serve as a form of promotion for next year's race. Lastly, the personal observations of the planning committee are also extremely useful in evaluating the race. Conduct a post-race meeting of planning committee members and ask for oral and written recommendations and/or suggestions for improvement. With this information in hand you are ready to start the process all over again as you prepare for next year's race.

## Summary

Of the 30 million runners in the United States, The Athletic Congress (TAC) estimated that 1.1 million ran in organized races in 1986. TAC estimated that 5,342 prominent races were conducted during the same year but is only one-half of all races actually held. The NRDC projects that the number of organized running races will increase at a rate of 5 percent annually.

Organizing a running event requires special planning in several program areas like safety, registration, timing/scoring and logistics. Safety is the first responsibility and priority of the race director. Safety guidelines for race directors include the provision of aid stations and emergency medical care, and adequate supervision (race marshalls). Aid stations with water and/or carbohydrate sports drinks should be positioned on the course every 2 kilometers and include safety marshalls with medical equipment and supplies. Racers under 18 years must have a parent or guardian sign the waiver form.

When designing the race course and location, the race site should have suitable terrain for running, adequate parking for the estimated number of racers/spectators, electricity, running water, and be accessible to special populations. Local parks, athletic fields and community centers are common race sites because they have these features. Arrangements must be made with local police to provide security and traffic control at intersections where high automobile volume may be a safety hazard.

The RRCA identified five items of considerable expense in race organization: printing, advertising, awards, refreshments and clerical-related services. Racer registration fees are typically used to offset a portion or the total operating expenditures.

Steps should be taken to make it as easy as possible for the runners to enroll in the race. Requiring pre-race day registration to participate in an race makes things less hectic on race day, but it also prevents those spontaneous recreators who decide that morning to run in the race from doing so. As many as 55 percent of the total number of runners can be gained through race-day registration. It is common practice to offer a reduced fee to those persons registering two weeks before the event (e.g., $8 pre-race, $12 race-day).

Direct mail is an important form of marketing running races. Mailing lists of runners who participated in other races may be obtained from organizers. It is also advised to hand out registration forms at the finish line of other races and to mail registration forms directly to local running clubs in the area.

For timing and scoring purposes, racers are typically categorized by age and gender. An example of an age categorization for a 10K running race would be: 9 years and under; 10-14; 15-19; 20-24; 25-29; 30-34; 35-39; 40-44; 45-49; 50-54; 55-59; 60 and above. Some race organizers are enlarging the number of winners by creating unique race categories such as family team categories, weight divisions, predicted time winners, door prize drawings, and costume contests.

To better identify racers in their respective age categories and gender divisions, race organizers utilize a color-coded race numbering system. Numbered race bibs often have a peel-off section where racer information (name, age, gender) is placed. As the racers finish, the information sticker is removed, and the finisher's time is written on it. The sticker is then placed on the corresponding age/gender division results poster. A manual back-up timing/scoring system with stop watches and place cards is also recommended.

The Athletic Congress (TAC) has recently developed an unique scoring system gaining popularity with race organizers based on finish times collected from numerous races over the years. Under this handicap system all racers are given a starting time handicap determined by TACSTATS/USA standards for age and gender. The advantage to the handicap system is that all racers have the chance to cross the finish line first regardless of age or gender.

Large numbers of human resources are needed to conduct a successful race, regardless of participant size. A small 5K running race (80 participants) may require up to 40 volunteers.

Thorough written evaluations and final race reports may offer a wealth of information in planning next year's race and therefore should not be overlooked. It is recommended that a variety of evaluation methods be employed. Consider implementing a post-race survey of participants through exit interviews, mail evaluation forms or both.

# References

Gjerdian, D. (1983). Race ownership. *Road Race Management*, 23(2).

Goodsen, R. N. & Hills, W. L. (1983). Organizational and administrative considerations involved in community running events. *Road Race Management*, 21(3).

Haggerty, T. & Paton, G. (1984). *Financial Management of Sport-Related Organizations*. Champaign, Illinois: Stipes Publishing.

Honikman, B. (1985). *TAC Times*. 5(1).

National Running Data Center (NRDC). (1982). *Race Director's Handbook*. Boulder, CO: NRDC.

Wong, G. (1991). Sports Law: The Theoretical Aspects, In B. L. Parkhouse (Ed.), *The Management of Sport*. St. Louis: Mosby-Year Book, Inc.

Thompson, S. (1984). Trends in race size. *Road Race Management*, 34(4).

Tinsley, H. (1984). Investments and returns. *Runner's World*, 21(1).

Turco, D. M. (1985). *An Investigation of Municipal Park/Recreation Department Organized Running Races in the United States* (Unpublished Masters Thesis). LaCrosse, WI: University of Wisconsin-LaCrosse.

Warner, P. (1984). The economic impact of the San Francisco Marathon. *Road Race Management*, 33(4).

# CHAPTER TEN
## Sport Sponsorship

Corporate sponsorships provide an organization with the money to fund a sporting event, advertisement to increase awareness, and sometimes even the human resources to help run the event. Sponsorships can be of great value to the sport agency but the agency must take careful measures when contracting with corporations to cover all the rights, responsibilities, and liabilities of each party.

## Promotional Licensing

Mullin and Sutton (1993) place sponsorship and other external contractual arrangements in sport under an umbrella term, "promotional licensing." Promotional licensing is the acquisition of rights to affiliate or associate with a product or event for the purpose of deriving benefits related to that affiliation or association. Such rights may include retail opportunities, purchase of media time, entitlement, or hospitality. Promotional licensing, as describe by Mullin, et. al., (1993) may include the following:

o The right to use a logo, name, trademark, and graphic representation signifying the purchasers connection with the product/event.

o The right to use various designations in connection with the product/event, such as "official sponsor."

o The right of entitlement to any event or facility.

o The right to an exlcusive association within a product or service category.

o The right to conduct certain promotional activities in conjunction with the licensing agreement, such as contests or sales-driven activities.


## Sponsorship Defined

Mullin and Sutton (1993) define sponsorship as the provision of resources (fiscal, human, media, and physical) by an organization directly to an event or activity in exchange for a direct association to the event or activity. The providing organization can then use the direct association to achieve either its corporate, marketing, or media objectives. Corporate sponsorship has also been defined as "an agreement in terms of which a sponsor provides some aid to the beneficiary which may be an association, a team, or an individual, to enable the latter to pursue some activity, and thereby derives the benefits contemplated in terms of promotion strategy" (Abratt & Grobler, 1989). Essentially, corporate sponsorship is an agreement between the sponsor and the sponsored to meet mutually agreed objectives.

There are various forms or types of sponsorship. Some corporations contribute money, equipment, human resources, or a combination of these forms of assistance. What is contributed depends on what the agency needs for the event and what thew corporation is willing to contribute. Also, some events can be fully sponsored by one corporation while another may require many sponsors with either equal or unequal representation.

## The Sponsorship Plan

This assignment has two purposes. The first is to learn about corporate sponsorship by doing research on an event/service and companies which are potential sponsors. The second purpose is to learn about marketing a sporting event by developing a sponsorship plan for a recreation/sport event/service.

You need to be creative and imaginative when trying to identify potential sponsors. Your first task is to develop a contact list by identifying as many businesses or companies as possible which may have an interest in sponsoring the event or service and which have the financial ability to be a sponsor. A good place to get information about a company is at the local Chamber of Commerce. Many business profiles are listed there. The best way to learn about a company is to get a copy of their annual report. Other good sources of information on companies are Moody's Manuals, Standard and Poor's Industry Surveys and various company directories.

Keep in mind that both the business and the event/service need to benefit from the sponsorship arrangement. Most businesses are interested in marketing and selling their products or services to potential customers. If a sporting event can provide a platform for this venture, then a successful relationship is possible. What has attracted sponsors in the past has been their potential to reach potential customers. Listed below are some questions which you need to answer before approaching a company as a sponsor:

## Getting Started

1. What are the demographics of my event/service? Who are the event's participants?

2. What are the demographics of the target company?

3. What type of product or service does the target company produce?

4. What are the general promotional approaches of the target company?

5. Where does the company stand versus the competition?

6. Has the company used sport or event sponsorship before? If yes, was the experience positive or negative? Has the company previously sponsored the event you are representing? Was the relationship positive?

7. Who makes the marketing decisions for the target company?

8. Why would this company want to sponsor my event/service?
   - a. increase sales
   - b. product sampling
   - c. store traffic
   - d. public/community relations
   - e. entertainment
   - f. promotional considerations
   - g. other (specify)

9. What possible controversies might result from this company's sponsorship of my event/service?

10. How will my event/service benefit from a sponsorship arrangement with this business?

## Steps to Successful Sport Sponsorship

I.  Design the Sporting Event with Sponsorship Opportunities
The Kodak Albuquerque International Balloon Fiesta conducts in-depth, on-site, spectator interviews to determine customer satisfaction. In 1992, survey data revealed that parents with young children were dissatisfied with the portable toilets on the Balloon Fiesta grounds as a place for diaper changing.

II. Secure Media Sponsors
Solicit media sponsors first. Once secured, they can promote the event through their normal media distribution channels.

III. Define Sponsorship Levels
Designate various levels of corporate support. If a corporation is providing your event with resources other than financial (i.e., labor, technical equipment, etc.) a market value should be placed on these resources.

IV. Distinguish Benefits of Sponsorship in Accord with Levels
Sponsors should receive benefits corresponding to their level of resources provided to the event. By no means should a company paying an event $500 receive the same benefits as a company paying $50,000.

V.  Assemble Sponsorship Proposal
At a minimum, a sponsorship proposal should contain the following information:
   - A. Event history
   - B. Sponsorship Levels
   - C. Benefits
   - D. Profile of event participants, spectators
   - E. Describe past media exposure
   - F. Listing of past sponsors

VI.     Identify Prospective Sponsors
        Your complete responses to the ten questions posed earlier in this
chapter will have thoroughly described prospective sponsors.

VII.    Contract with Sponsors
        Identify the corporate decision-makers and seek them out.  Be
persistent and patient.

VIII.   Evaluate the Effectiveness of Sponsorships
        Examples of sponsorship evaluations include measuring the event's
economic impacts, quantifying sponor's media mentions, and conducting
spectator recall/recognition tests.

IX.     Provide Post-event Report
        Provide each sponsor with an event wrap-up and results of the
sponsor evaluation.  If an annual event, provide the sponsor with the
opportunity to renew their sponsorship in advance of other direct
competitors.


## Sponsor Plan Assignment

        Select a sport/recreation event/service of your choice and prepare a
sponsorship plan featuring the following components:

1. Event/Service - Description, history, markets, media coverage

2. Sponsorship opportunities - benefits to sponsor

3. Levels of sponsorship - Resources provided by sponsor to event/service
in exchange for benefits

4. Descriptions of prospective sponsors

5. Action plan (prioritized time line) for implementation of sponsor plan


## Benefits to Sport Organization

        An agency receives many benefits from using a corporate sponsor.
The most obvious benefit is financial assistance.  Some corporations have
separate funds that include amounts available for charities, special events,
and advertising or they may contribute the money to receive a tax write-off.
In 1990, the top three corporate sponsors were Anheuser-Busch at $175
million, General Motors at $150 million, and Phillip Morris at $128 million.
        Corporations often promote the events they sponsor.  Another
benefit of corporate sponsorship is the enhanced reputation the event
receives as a result of the corporation's affiliation.  This may lead to more

participants, spectators, and sponsors that otherwise would not have been associated with the event.

## Benefits to Corporations

Corporate sponsorships totaled $96 billion in 1993 and are projected to grow 15% in 1994. Sporting events are the most popular options for sponsors, comprising 67 percent of all sponsor dollars.

What Does Sport Have to Offer a Sponsor?
+ Media mentions
+ Logo display
+ Signage
+ Hospitality
+ Product sampling
+ Stage or venue
+ Advertising in program

Why Do Companies Sponsor Sport?
+ Enhance market's perception of product (image)
+ Merchandising opportunities (sales)
+ Community pride and involvement
+ Hospitality opportunities
+ Lifestyle identification

Corporations also receive many advantages for sponsoring sporting events. As previously stated, sponsorships may be used as a tax write-off or as another way to promote the corporation's product and/or image. Other advantages are their ability to test new products or promote existing one at the event through samples, coupons, drawings, and displays.

Corporations benefit from their sponsorship as much as the event organization because of the publicity it receives that leads to public recognition of respectability, responsibility and status. Abratt and Grobler (1989) claim corporate sponsorship has a positive effect on consumers, the trade, and a corporation's employees. Among consumers, it can improve brand awareness and image, encourage trial and promote consumer loyalty. State Abratt and Grobler, "a good program can provide the trade with a special sales tool, serve as a spring boars from merchandising and promotion themes, and form the foundation for some exciting incentive and motivation programs." They add that a corporation's employees, particularly at tobacco and alcohol companies, receive a great sense of pride and unity from event sponsorship. Corporate sponsorship can be a chance to get press and television coverage of the company name where tobacco and some alcohol advertisements are banned.

The following sponsorship plan for an in-line skating race illustrates the various levels of sponsorship and their corresponding benefits to the sponsor.

---

# EXCLUSIVE DAY AND EVENT SPONSORSHIPS

An Exclusive Sponsorship is one Sponsor featured exclusively for one day. All packages include: Signage at Balloon Fiesta Park, listing or mention in pre-Fiesta publicity, schedules and brochures. • As a designated Exclusive Product Sponsor, KAIBF grants to Sponsor an exclusive license to use the phrase "The Official_____" of the Kodak Albuquerque International Balloon Fiesta as well as the Official Logo until January 31st of the following year. • The term Exclusive shall exclude any direct product involvement of a company, individual and/or entity deemed directly competitive to the above named Sponsor at Balloon Fiesta Park, but shall not prevent KAIBF from offering Balloon Sponsorships to any entity or individual deemed directly competitive to Sponsor.

## EXCLUSIVE WEEKEND SPONSORSHIPS First Saturday or First Sunday

Choose sponsorship of the first Saturday or Sunday, and you reach the largest crowds the Balloon Fiesta has to offer. Anticipation and enthusiasm are at their peak as spectators explore the wonders of this unique event. No sponsorship offers greater penetration or long-term awareness.

• Two balloons carrying Sponsor banners during scheduled Fiesta events (weather permitting)
• Sponsor balloons will launch first to open day's events, accompanied by the National Anthem

• Balloon ride for four people
• Full-page color ad in Official Program (Value: $2500)
• Ten Sponsor parking passes
• 250 Sponsor pins
• Ten tickets to each social function
• 20' x 20' Corporate Hospitality Tent in Corporate Village
• Ten Sponsor jackets and two pilot jackets with corporate name/logo
• Ten Sponsor Hospitality Tent passes
• Exclusive product designation
• Investment: $50,000

## SHAPE UP! Special Shape Rodeo Sponsorship

No other single event is as widely anticipated as the Special Shape Rodeo. There's practically no limit to the size or creativity of the Special Shape balloon, from bottles to ships, cows to motorcycles. Special Shape balloons are only limited by the imagination of the builder, and this world-famous rodeo includes some fabulous themes.

• Two balloons carrying Sponsor banner during scheduled Fiesta events (weather permitting)

• Full-page color ad in Official Program (Value: $2500)
• Eight Sponsor parking passes
• 250 Sponsor pins
• Eight tickets to each social function
• 20' x 20' Corporate Hospitality Tent in Corporate Village
• Eight Sponsor Hospitality Tent passes
• Eight Sponsor jackets and two pilot jackets with corporate name/logo
• Exclusive product designation
• Investment: $50,000

## ALL KEYED UP! Exclusive Key Grab Day Sponsorship

Key Grab Day is one of the Balloon Fiesta's few competitive events, with the winner taking home a brand new automobile. The Key Grab is a game of pilot skill and reckoning, challenging the balloon to fly toward a 30-foot pole with a set of car keys attached to the top. The first balloon team to pick the keys off the pole wins the car. Key Grab Day is always attended to capacity.

• One balloon carrying Sponsor banner during scheduled Fiesta events (weather permitting)
• Sponsor balloon will launch first to open day's events, accompanied by the National Anthem
• Balloon ride for four people

• Full-page color ad in Official Program (Value: $2500)
• Eight Sponsor parking passes
• 250 Sponsor pins
• Eight tickets to each social function
• 20' x 20' Corporate Hospitality Tent in Corporate Village
• Eight Sponsor Hospitality Tent passes
• Eight Sponsor jackets and one pilot jacket with corporate name/logo
• Field signage and display on field
• Exclusive product designation
• Investment: $40,000

## EXCLUSIVE WEEKEND SPONSORSHIPS Second Saturday or Second Sunday

Mass ascensions always attract more spectators, so a weekend day sponsorship is a sure winner! Final weekend sponsorships will leave a lasting impression with people remembering this year and anticipating next year's event.

• Two balloons carrying Sponsor banner during scheduled Fiesta events (weather permitting)
• Sponsor balloons will launch first to open the day's events, accompanied by the National Anthem.
• Balloon ride for four people

• Full-page color ad in Official Program (Value: $2500)
• Six Sponsor parking passes
• 250 Sponsor pins
• Six tickets to each social function
• 20' x 20' Corporate Hospitality Tent in Corporate Village
• Six Sponsor Hospitality Tent passes
• Six Sponsor jackets and two pilot jackets with corporate name/logo
• Exclusive product designation
• Investment: $30,000

## LIGHT UP! *Balloon Glow Sponsorship*

Balloon Glow fills the twilight sky with a kinetic rainbow of brilliant color that defies description. At about 7 PM, pilots of more than 300 stationary balloons ignite their propane burners to fill each envelope with dazzling color. The effect is a hundred times more brilliant than the most spectacular of sunsets. Balloon Glow never fails to make the evening news around the nation.

- One balloon carrying Sponsor banner during scheduled Fiesta events (weather permitting)

- Balloon ride for four people
- Full-page color ad in Official Program (Value: $2500)
- Six Sponsor parking passes
- 250 Sponsor pins
- Six tickets to each social function
- 20' x 20' Corporate Hospitality Tent in Corporate Village
- Six Sponsor Hospitality Tent passes
- Six Sponsor jackets and one pilot jacket with corporate name/logo
- Exclusive product designation
- Investment: $30,000

## NIGHT MAGIC *Glow Sponsorship*

Night Magic will be held the second weekend and provides a powerful additional draw. Night Magic features 100+ balloons in a spectacular glow of evening color. By popular demand, Night Magic has become one of the Balloon Fiesta's traditional annual events.

- One balloon carrying Sponsor banner during scheduled Fiesta events (weather permitting)
- Balloon ride for two people

- 1/2-page color ad in Official Program (Value: $1500)
- Four Sponsor parking passes
- 250 Sponsor pins
- Four tickets to each social function
- Four Sponsor Hospitality Tent passes
- Four Sponsor jackets and one pilot jacket with corporate name/logo
- Exclusive product designation
- Investment: $25,000

## MID-WEEK FANTASY *Wednesday Mass Ascension Sponsorship*

Nothing can equal the sight of hundreds of balloons inflating and lifting off in a lyrical display of shape, color and motion. The field is always crowded to capacity before a mass ascension, with plenty of interplay between spectators and participants.

- Two balloons carrying Sponsor banner during scheduled Fiesta events (weather permitting)
- Sponsor balloons will launch first to open day's events, accompanied by the National Anthem
- Balloon ride for four people
- 1/2-page color ad in Official Program (Value: $1500)

- Six sponsor parking passes
- 250 Sponsor pins
- Six tickets to each social function
- Six Sponsor Hospitality Tent passes
- Six Sponsor jackets and two pilot jackets with corporate name/logo
- Opportunity to distribute promotional materials at the admission gates. (Sponsor to provide promotional materials to KAIBF by September 1, 1994)
- Exclusive product designation
- Investment: $25,000

## A DAY OF YOUR OWN *Monday or Tuesday Sponsorships*

This is your opportunity to sponsor a full day of Balloon Fiesta activities at a truly fantastic price. The excitement of the crowd is palpable, thanks to free interplay between spectators and crews. This means your sponsorship is noted...and remembered.

- One balloon carrying Sponsor banner during scheduled Fiesta events (weather permitting)
- Sponsor balloon will launch first to open day's events, accompanied by the National Anthem
- Balloon ride for four people

- 1/2-page color ad in Official Program (Value: $1500)
- Four sponsor parking passes
- 250 Sponsor pins
- Four tickets to each social function
- Four Sponsor Hospitality Tent passes
- Four Sponsor jackets and two pilot jackets with corporate name/logo
- Opportunity to distribute promotional materials at the admission gates. (Sponsor to provide promotional materials to KAIBF by September 1, 1994)
- Exclusive product designation
- Cost: $20,000 each day

# ONE-OF-A-KIND SPONSORSHIPS

## THE CALL OF THE HUNT Chase Vehicle Sponsorship

Aside from balloons themselves, chase vehicles are the most visible participants at the Balloon Fiesta. Each balloon is accompanied by a chase vehicle whose crew is charged with recovering balloon and occupants wherever they touch down. This means chase vehicles are seen everywhere in greater Albuquerque during the course of the event. You can't get more visible than that.

Chase vehicles fly your corporate flag for the entire event...and long afterwards at smaller balloon events throughout the year.

- Sponsorship of a balloon (See "Individual Balloon Sponsorships")
- 3' x 4' flag for each chase vehicle. Each of 1,000 flags will carry your name and logo, official Kodak Albuquerque International Balloon Fiesta logo and "Official Chase Vehicle" designation
- Balloon rides for two people
- 1/2-page color ad in Official Program (Value: $1500)
- Investment: $25,000

## TRAVEL IN LEISURE Park N' Ride Sponsorship

With event attendance approaching two million, more and more spectators are choosing the easy way to attend Balloon Fiesta during peak weekend hours: Park N' Ride. This service enhances the balloon experience by minimizing hassle, and thanks to liberal bus signage and on-site ID, they'll have your company to thank.

- Sponsorship of a balloon (See "Individual Balloon Sponsorships")
- Field signage at bus entrances/exits at Balloon Fiesta Park
- Signage on Albuquerque Sun Tran buses (side panels)

- Promotional coverage on radio and TV (two week campaign)
- Couponing and other promotional opportunities
- Four Sponsor parking passes, four tickets to all social functions, four passes to Sponsor Hospitality Tent
- Balloon ride for two people
- 1/2-page color ad in Official Program (Value: $1500)
- Two Sponsor jackets and one pilot jacket with corporate name/logo
- Investment: $25,000

## THROUGH THE EYES OF A CHILD Children's Balloon Explorium Sponsorship

The Children's Balloon Explorium is a wonder to behold for children. Why does a balloon fly? How can you control a balloon? The answers to these and other simple physics questions are delivered in a fun, interactive way. Kids learn and experience the joy of ballooning.

- One balloon banner flown during all scheduled Fiesta events (weather permitting)
- Balloon ride for two people
- Two Sponsor jackets and one pilot jacket with corporate name/logo

- Four Sponsor parking passes, four tickets to all social functions, four passes to Sponsor Hospitality Tent
- Pre-Fiesta publicity on TV, radio, newspaper and school publications
- 1/2-page color ad in Official Program (Value: $1500)
- Signage on 30' x 40' Balloon Explorium tent
- Directional signage to Balloon Explorium
- Volunteer staffing for tent and exhibits
- Opportunity for sampling, couponing and cross promotions
- Investment: $15,000

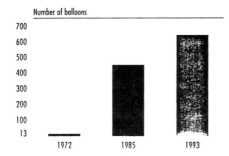

Number of balloons

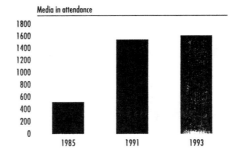

Media in attendance

162

# MEDIA TOWER AND HOSPITALITY SPONSORSHIPS

## HIGH LEVEL EXPOSURE *Media Tower ID and sponsorship*

The Media Tower acts as the focal point of Balloon Fiesta, a highly visible landmark which presents your Corporate Logo to an estimated 1.6 million people during the nine-day event, as well as untold millions of TV viewers!

• Signage on the Media Tower, visible to spectators and TV viewers around the world
• Sponsorship of a balloon (See "Individual Balloon Sponsorships")

• Balloon ride for two people
• 1/2-page color ad in Official Program (Value: $1500)
• Two tickets to all social functions
• Two passes to Sponsor Hospitality Tent
• Two Sponsor parking passes
• Two Sponsor jackets and one pilot jacket with corporate name/logo
• Investment: $10,000

## CORPORATE HOSPITALITY TENT *(When available)*

Your own limited-access island of refreshment and relaxation away from the crowds, the Corporate Hospitality Tent is an ideal way to entertain your invited guests and special clients.

• 20' x 20' tent in Corporate Village, an exclusive, secured area provided for you and your corporate clients. Tent is tastefully appointed and may include your product display or introduction of a new product. Includes private patio area with attractive landscaping.
• Investment: $6,000

## FIESTA HOSPITALITY TENT *(Available for individual events)*

This is your opportunity to entertain clients right on the balloon field, in a limited-access corporate village setting with private patio and landscaping.

• 20' x 40' tent, tastefully appointed (Sponsor provides own catering)
• Investment: $1,000 per event

## SPONSOR HOSPITALITY TENT

Lend your good name to the Hospitality Tent which all other sponsors will use throughout the event! This is The Fiesta's largest hospitality center, and is offered to all sponsors and accredited representatives.

• Larger tent with the following amenities: patio furniture inside and out, linens and centerpieces, telephones, landscaping with grass, flowers and plants

• Continental breakfast, light lunches and cocktails served daily. (Food and beverage service prepared and served by Co-Sponsor)
• Full-page color ad in Official Program
• Sponsorship of a balloon (See "Individual Balloon Sponsor-ships")
• Investment: $15,000

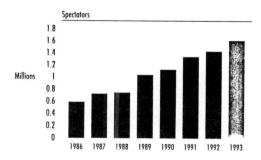

163

# IN-LINE EXTREME '96
*An Inaugural Event to Benefit the*

## EVENT SPONSORSHIP PACKAGES

### LEVEL I - Ultimate Sponsor Package
Commitment of resources (monetary/goods/services) totaling over $5000 by March 1, 1996

#### SPONSOR BENEFITS
+ **Title Sponsor** - Business shares in the name of the event (i.e., "Name of Business" In-Line Extreme '96)
+ **Exclusivity** - No other direct business competitor will permitted to co-sponsor the event.
+ Designated "Official ( your business' "product/service") Sponsor of In-Line Extreme '96"
+ Business name and logo is placed on official race t-shirt and registration forms, flyers, start and finish banners.
+ Complimentary race registration for up to 20 employees.
+ Opportunity for business display and product sampling at the event.

### LEVEL II - Presenting Sponsor Package
Sponsor underwrites cost of Extreme Games events or other event peripherals by March 1, 1996 (Dollar amount may vary).
+ **Exclusivity** - No other direct business competitor will be permitted to co-sponsor the event.
+ Designated "Official ( your business' "product/service") Sponsor of In-Line Extreme '96 (event peripheral)."
+ Business name and logo is placed on official race t-shirt and registration forms and flyers.
+ One complimentary race registration for every $100 sponsored.
+ Opportunities for product sampling; promotional tie-ins

### LEVEL III - Excellent Sponsor Package
Commitment of resources (monetary/goods/services) between $500 and $5000 by March 1, 1996.
+ **Exclusivity** - No other direct business competitor will be permitted to co-sponsor the event.
+ Designated "Official ( your business' "product/service") Sponsor of In-Line Extreme '96"
+ Business name and logo is placed on official race t-shirt and registration forms and flyers.
+ One complimentary race registration for every $100 sponsored.
+ Opportunities for product sampling; promotional tie-ins

## LEVEL IV - Cool Sponsor Package
Commitment of resources (monetary/goods/services) between $100 and $500 by March 1, 1996.
+ Business name and logo is placed on official race t-shirt and promotional materials.
+ One complimentary race registration for every $100 sponsored.
+ Opportunities for coupon and promotional tie-ins.

## LEVEL V - Skate Sponsor Package
Commitment of resources (monetary/goods/services) up to $100.
+ Business receives recognition (name and logo) on promotional materials (i.e., flyers, registration forms).
+ Business receives one complimentary race registration

---

## Sport Sponsorship Trends
A recent trend in corporate sponsorships is the heavy emphasis on sporting events whether local, national, or international in scope. In 1988, approximately 70 percent of all sponsorship money was spent on sports (Friedman, 1988)  In 1989, 25 of the 39 televised Professional Golf Association (PGA) events were named for sponsors, as were 17 major college football bowls (Macnow, 1989). Reasons for this trend are that the participants may use the corporation's products, a wide variety of people can be reached because of the various sporting events, and the corporation's name may be used on event brochures, signs, radio and television commercials, and some players' uniforms or equipment. Because there are so many corporations sponsoring various sporting events, corporations need to promote and research the event they want to sponsor in order to insure that their sponsorship will be effective. Lisa Ukman, editor of *Special Events Report*, suggests that any company paying for a national sponsorship be prepared to spend at least three times the cost of the sponsorship on promotion.

## Considerations in Sponsorship
Besides basing a decision about using corporate sponsorship on how much money can be obtained, an organization should check into other characteristics. First, determine if the event and the sponsor are compatible. If the event is intended to improve participants' cardiovascular system, an organization would not seek Marlboro as a sponsor. Also, if an organization has multiple sponsors, the sponsors should be compatible to each other as well. For instance, if Coke is a large sponsor of an event, they may not appreciate if the event's concession stands sold Pepsi. Corporations need to consider the logistics of the event. They must ask questions about security, crowd control, seating, and if the event will draw the desired crowd. Corporations need to make sure that the event draws a crowd that is not only sizable, but also holds the right demographic

165

characteristics to suit the company. The other characteristics that must be carefully examined are the legal aspects that are found in a sponsorship contract between both parties.

## Contracts

A written contract is critical in event sponsorship. The document must detail many aspects of the agreement so the parties involved will realize their limitations, rights, and responsibilities. A contract clarifies the rights that the sponsor is receiving and those the organizer is retaining, it preserves "sponsor exclusivity," protects any trademarks, and protects both parties from unwanted liability.

When designing a contract for sponsorship, the length and detail of the contract depends upon the involvement of the sponsor. The more money, promotion, and number of events that the sponsor is involved with, the longer and more detailed will be the contract. The following section explains the basic components that should be covered in a contract. Figure 1 contains an example of a sponsorship agreement.

1. The name of the parties involved, the beginning and ending dates of the contract, the name of the event, the location of the site, and the signatures of each party are required of each contract in order to be valid.

2. There is usually a paragraph explaining the sponsor's status. This paragraph states how many sponsors are involved with the event. If there is only one sponsor, the organizer states that he will not allow a product of one of the sponsor's competitors to be used/promoted at the event. This situation is referred to as *exclusivity*.

3. A section of the contract specifies the limits on using each parties' trademark in any form of advertisement whether it be television, signs, banners, brochures, products, etc. Strict limits are usually enforced on television advertisements and on the size, amount, and placement of certain signs and banners.

4. The sponsorship fee is stated in a dollar amount and how and when it is to be paid. The fee can be paid in one lump sum or by installments. A letter of credit is often required. This letter assured the organizer of payment and is usually distributed by some type of financial institution.

A rebate should also be given when "Acts of God" (i.e., weather, flood, fire, or any other situation beyond the control of the parties) occur. Either all or part of the fee is refunded. If the event does not take place, a full refund would be issued; if a portion of the event is cancelled, only a proportionate amount of the sponsorship fee is returned.

5. Merchandising rights state that any item sold related to the event must be suitable in appearance, quality, and for the intended purpose. An additional statement is made to express the proportionate share that each party will receive of the profits from sales.

If the sponsor manufactures its own event-related merchandise, merchantability will come into effect. *Merchantability* is an implied warranty by a manufacturer which implies that the goods are reasonably suited for the purpose for which they are sold, therefore the sponsor is held liable for the products.

6. If an event is more than a one time event, a *renewal option* may be included with certain limitations.

7. Both parties are required to carry a *Comprehensive General Liability Insurance Policy* for a stated dollar amount and a number of years depending on the circumstances of the event.

8. Certain situations may be listed and if violated, the sponsor or event organizer would have the right to terminate the agreement. Common instances occur during bankruptcy filings, trademark violations, or materially misstated representations in the contract. Another termination situation would be if one of the parties defaults on a provision in the agreement and it is not reconciled within 30 days. Materially means that the mistake was large in proportion to the contract, and cure means that the defaulting party would have a chance to correct the provision (Reed, 1990, 33-50).

## Liability

Organizers are generally more active than sponsors when conducting the event, and are more often held liable for injuries that occur to participants and spectators. Organizers must follow through on their duty of standard due care. This duty states that the organizer should make sure there are no "unreasonable risks" that may result in an injury to a participant or spectator. *Unreasonable risks* include any risks that are not normal or ordinary to an activity (Reed, 1990). An example of an unreasonable risk would be an attack of a cycler by a guard dog during an organized bicycle road race. *Due care* means the care that an ordinary person would apply to a situation. This could include checking the running paths before a race or checking.

Organizers are only liable to injured parties if the following four criteria exist. First, the organizer must have duty or obligation to conform to a certain standard. Second, the organizer must have failed to meet the standard (known as a breach). Third, the injury must have been connected with the organizer's conduct. Lastly, the complaining party must prove that an actual injury or damage of property occurred and it is compensational by law.

## Waivers

Waivers or release forms can release organizers from some liability to event participants. These forms state that a participant agrees not to hold the organizer liable for injuries resulting from the event. There are four guidelines that event organizers should follow when using waivers. First, the form should have large lettering, be easy to read, and be a separate document. Second, the form should state the parties that are being released of liability. Third, the risks being waived should be stated. Fourth, organizers should instruct all persons administering these forms that they are responsible for informing participant about the nature of the release. The guidelines must be strictly followed and under no circumstances may an organizer be released from the standard duty of care (Reed, 1990).

Figure 1

## Sample Short Form
## Sponsorship Letter Agreement

Sponsor
Address
City/State/Zip

Dear _____:

This will confirm the terms and conditions on which *(name of Sponsor)* ("you") have agreed to sponsor the *(name of Event)* (the "Event) organized by *(name of Organizer)* ("us").

1. We shall use our best efforts to conduct and promote *(describe)*. [We will use our best efforts to cause the Event, date and place to be sanctioned by *(name of Sanctioning Organization if any)*. The failure of the Event to be sanctioned shall not, however, void this Agreement.]

2. We hereby grant you the right to be [an] [the] official Sponsor of the Event. You shall have the right to use the name of the Event [and the name of trademark)] as well as the names and likenesses of participants in advertising prior to and for _____ months after the Event in connection with your sponsorship, provided the names of participants are not used as an endorsement of any product or service. All such materials are subject to our prior written approval, which shall not be unreasonably withheld.

3. We shall use our best efforts to provide you with {signage at the Event, etc.].

4. We shall provide you with _____ free tickets.

5.  We shall give you credit as [a] sponsor in all advertising and promotional materials prepared by us in the following form:
"_____."

6.  If we produce a videotape of the Event for home distribution or broadcast or other use, we will use our best efforts to provide you with sponsorship credit therein.

7.  In consideration of all rights granted you hereunder, you will pay us $_____, payable _____.

8.  We shall provide a comprehensive general liability insurance covering the participants and the crowd in the face amount of $_____ and shall cause you to be named as an insured thereon.

9.  You recognize that we own all rights to the Event and you agree not to sponsor a similar event within (*number*) miles of (*site*) for a period of (*number of days or months*) from the date of the Event.

10.  We shall have the right to use your trademarks in advertising and promoting the Event, including on any merchandise authorized by us in connection with the Event.  Any merchandise produced by us shall be of high quality consistent with your outstanding public image and you shall have the right to approve the same in writing in advance, provided that such approval shall not be unreasonably withheld.

11.  Each party represents and warrants that it is free to enter into this Agreement without violating the rights of any person, that its trademarks or trade names of any person and that it will comply with all laws and regulations pertinent to its business.

12.  In the event that the Event does not take place due to any cause beyond the reasonable control of the parties, this Agreement shall terminate and our only obligation shall be to return you the fee paid us hereunder less any direct out-of-pocket expenses incurred by us prior to the date of termination.

13.  This Agreement does not constitute a partnership or joint venture or principal-agent relationship between us.  This Agreement may not be assigned by either party.  It shall be governed by the laws of the State of (state).  It is complete and represents the entire agreement between the parties.

If this accurately sets forth our Agreement, please sign below and return a copy to me.

Sincerely,

Event Organizer

By: _____

Agreed and Accepted this _____ day of _____, 19_____


_____
Sponsor

## Controversy in Sport Sponsorship
*Alcohol and Tobacco Sponsors*

    A growing number of people are opposing certain sponsors, particularly alcohol and tobacco sponsors.  An important issue facing event organizers is whether or not alcohol and tobacco advertisers should be banned from sporting events.  Some towns, such as Huntington Beach, California, are taking matters into their own hands by combining its longtime ban on alcohol consumption at the beach with a new ban on alcohol advertising (Brown, 1991).  Hunington Beach, which hosts many surf and beach volleyball tournaments, has experienced numerous cases of violence because of alcohol.  Major brewers have found great marketing opportunities at beach locations where they sponsor professional surfing and volleyball tours and advertise using banners towed by planes and boats.  Even the volleyball nets feature the brewer's logo.  The National Basketball Association's Minnesota Timberwolves franchise has refused to accept cigarette advertising in their new arena, the Target Center.

    The Virginia Slims Tennis Tournament sponsored by Phillip Morris, is currently one of the biggest and most controversial tournaments to be sponsored by a tobacco company.  Athletes who compete in the tournament are accused of lending their image to tobacco companies and showcasing their talents in front of a sign promoting cigarettes.  The trophy that Virginia Slims champions receive depicts the figure of a sleek and sophisticated woman holding a tennis racquet in one hand and a cigarette in the other.  Critics contend there is a definite contradiction of a cigarette company associating its name with a young, healthy athlete, especially since most of the players on the tour do not smoke.

    Tennis tournaments are not the only sporting events the tobacco industry has targeted.  Soccer, for example, offers cigarette makers overseas popularity, particularly at a time when they are trying to step up their Third World trade.  Camel cigarettes, manufactured by R. J. Reynolds, was one of four major sponsors of the 1986 World Cup in Mexico.  The company put up 23-foot high Camel signs in 12 stadiums in nine Mexican cities.  Baseball is another sport that cigarette companies sponsor.  Cigarette companies have advertisements in 22 of the 24 Major League ballparks in the United States, typically in spots that have the most broadcast coverage.  In New York's Shea Stadium, the camera near the visiting team dugout used to capture players leading off first base, frames the player with the Marlboro sign in left centerfield.  A third alternative for sport sponsorship is auto racing. Since 1971, the R. J. Reynolds Tobacco Company has been the principle sponsor of the National Association for Stock Car Auto Racing's (NASCAR) premier circuit, the Winston Cup series. Sponsors of auto racing can paint their name and logo all over the car, driver, and sidelines. Other tobacco company sponsored events have included Lucky Strike bowling, the Winston Rodeo, RJR Cup Seniors Golf, and Benson and Hedges on Ice.

Recent action taken by groups opposed to alcohol and tobacco sponsors may make sponsorships for these companies difficult. Primarily dealing with cigarette sponsorship, action groups are making progress in their anti-tobacco campaigns. Doctors Ought to Care (DOC) has persuaded co-sponsors to withdraw support for Virginia Slims tournaments and has forced changes of venue at other events. DOC has also pressured the U.S. Attorney General to enforce the broadest possible interpretation of the Public Health Smoking Act of 1969, which banned cigarette advertising from television. Presently, Canada bans *all* tobacco advertising and advocacy groups are seeking similar legislation in the U.S.

Congress has considered several bills which impact cigarette advertising. These bills have called for the termination of existing tobacco brand sponsorship of events and prohibits cigarette advertising in sports stadiums. Such legislation has been enacted in Canada, France, Sweden, and Norway.Such legislation has been enacted in Canada, France, Sweden, and Norway.

## Summary

Corporate sponsorship is an agreement between the sponsor and the sponsored to meet mutually agreed objectives. In 1990, the top three corporate sponsors were Anheuser-Busch at $175 million, General Motors at $150 million, and Phillip Morris at $128 million. The four main forms of corporate sponsorship are money, equipment, human resources, or a combination of these forms of assistance.

Corporations receive many advantages for sponsoring sporting events. Sponsorships may be used as a tax write-off or as another way to promote the corporation's product and/or image. Other advantages are their ability to test new products or promote existing one at the event through samples, coupons, drawings, and displays.

A written contract is critical in event sponsorship. The document must detail many aspects of the agreement so the parties involved will realize their limitations, rights, and responsibilities.

An important issue facing sport event organizers is whether or not alcohol and tobacco advertisers should be banned from sporting events. The Virginia Slims Tennis Tournament sponsored by Phillip Morris, is currently one of the biggest and most controversial tournaments to be sponsored by a tobacco company. Athletes who compete in the tournament are accused of lending their image to tobacco companies and showcasing their talents in front of a sign promoting cigarettes. Doctors Ought to Care (DOC) has persuaded co-sponsors to withdraw support for Virginia Slims tournaments and has forced changes of venue at other events. DOC has also pressured the U.S. Attorney General to enforce the broadest possible interpretation of the Public Health Smoking Act of 1969, which banned cigarette advertising from television. Presently, Canada bans *all* tobacco advertising and advocacy groups are seeking similar legislation in the U.S. The U. S. Congress is considering in 1992 several bills in the next session which will impact cigarette advertising.

## References

Abratt, R. & Grobler, P. (1989). The evaluation of sports sponsorships. *International Journal of Advertising*, 8(1): 351-362.

Johnston, W. (August, 1990) Sponsors. *Forbes*, 68-70.

Macnow, G. (1989). Sport tie-ins help firms score. *Nation's Business* (September, 1989), 36-38.

Reed, M. H. (1990). *The IEG Legal Guide to Sponsorship*. Chicago: International Events Group.

# APPENDIX A
## Sports Associations

*Youth Baseball*
Little League Baseball, Inc.
P.O. Box 3485
Williamsport, PA  17701
(717) 326-1921
FAX:  (412) 326-1074
http://netplaza.com/plaza/public/1024/welcome.html

Babe Ruth Baseball and Softball
P.O. Box 5000
1770 Brunswick Avenue
Trenton, NJ  08638
(609) 695-1434
FAX:  (609) 695-2505

PONY Baseball, Inc.
P.O. Box 225
15301
(412) 225-1060
FAX:  (412) 225-9852

DIXIE Baseball, Inc.
215 Watauga LaneWashington, PA
P.O. Box 222
Lookout Mountain, TN  37350
(615) 821-6811

American Legion Baseball
700 N. Pennsylvania
Indianapolis, IN  46204
(317) 635-8411
FAX:  (317) 635-8411. Ext. 401
Mailing:          P.O. Box 1055
                  Indianapolis, IN  46206

*Adult Softball*
Amateur Softball Association
2801 Northeast 50th Street
Oklahoma City, OK  73111
(405) 424-5266
FAX:  (405) 424-3855

*Bicycling*
United States Cycling Federation
1750 East Boulder Street
Colorado Springs, CO  80909
(719) 578-4581   Colorado Springs, CO  80909
FAX:  (719) 578-4628

World Bicycle Polo Federation
P.O. Box 1039
Bailey, Colorado  80421
(303) 892-8801

*Circular Zoneball*
Stratball Sports, Inc.
P.O. Box 300
Marstons Mills, Massachusetts 02648
(508) 428-1914

*Golf*
Professional Golfers' Association of America (PGA)
100 Avenue of Champions
P.O. Box 109601
Palm Beach Gardens, FL 33410
(407) 624-8400
FAX: (407) 624-8452

Ladies' Professional Golf Association
2570 Volusia Avenue, Suite B
Daytona Beach, FL 32114
(904) 254-8800
FAX: (904) 254-4755

*Racquetball*
American Amateur Racquetball Association
815 North Weber
Colorado Springs, CO 80903
(719) 635-5396
FAX: (719) 635-0685
http://emporium.turnpike.net/~cyberguy/magaz.html

*Running*

The Athletic Congress
One Hoosier Dome
Indianapolis, IN 46225
(317) 261-0500
FAX: (317) 261-0481
Mailing: P.O. Box 120
Indianapolis, IN 46225

Road Runners Club of America
629 S. Washington Street
Alexandria, VA 22314
(703) 836-0558
http://www.rrca.org/~rrca/

*Skateboarding*
National Skateboarding Association
P.O. Box 1916
Vista, CA 92083
(619) 941-1844
FAX: (619) 945-7893
Amateur Office: P.O. Box 30444
San Bernadino, CA 92413
(714) 883-3581

*Soccer*
American Youth Soccer Organization
5403 West 138th Street
Hawthorne, CA 90250

(213) 643-6455
FAX: (213) 643-5310
http://www.soccer.org/

*Tennis*
United States Tennis Association
1212 Avenue of the Americas
New York, NY 10036
(212) 302-3322
FAX: (212) 764-1838

*Triathlon*
Triathlon Federation/USA
3595 E. Fountain Blvd., F-1
Colorado Springs, CO 80910
(719) 597-9090
FAX: (719) 597-2121
Mailing: P.O. Box 15820
Colorado Springs, CO 80910
http://www.trinfo.com/trifed/

*Ultimate Frisbee*
Ultimate Frisbee Players Association
P.O. Box 2331
Silver City, New Mexico 88062
(505) 388-3111

*Volleyball*
United States Volleyball Association
3595 E. Fountain Blvd.
Colorado Springs, CO 80910-1740
(719) 597-8300
FAX: (719) 597-6307

**Other Sport Associations**
National Intramural Sports Association (NIRSA)
Gill Coliseum, Room 221
Oregon State University
Corvallis, Oregon 97331

National Sporting Goods Association
1699 Wall Street
Mt. Prospect, Illinois 60056
(708) 439-4000
FAX: (708) 439-0111

# Internet Sport and Recreation Sites

Bowling Page
http://www.rpi.edu/~miller3?bowling.html/

Sport and Recreation Page
http://www.bf.rmit.edu.au/~s9410536/sport.html

Various Hockey League Pages
http://www.gnn.com/gnn/metal/sport/hockey/various.html/

Skiing And Snowboarding
http://www.azstarnet.com/~goclimb/skihome.html

Volksmarch and Walking index
http://www.teleport.com:80/~walking?

USA Volleyball Home Page
http://www.volleyball.org/usav/index.html

# GLOSSARY

*Bracket* - The lines used in a tournament chart to show opposing players or teams.

*Bye* - A situation in a tournament where a team does not have an opponent and is advanced to the next round. No win is credited unless the team wins the next game (bye).

*Challenge* - Invitation to engage in a match or contest.

*Default* - A failure to begin or complete a match that has been scheduled or started. May be accidental.

*Disqualification* - Inability of a participant to continue involvement in an activity because of a rule infraction or misconduct.

*Division* - A larger participating component of a program containing one or more leagues grouped under a logical classification.

*Draw Sheet* - An official chart listing tournament participants and their individual assignments in the first round.

*Forfeit* - The loss of a sport event because of a violation of sport rules.

*Handicap* - An artificial disadvantage that can be the result of skill levels, age, weight, etc., which tends to equalize competition.

*League* - Grouping of teams of like ability and interest into compatible competitive play units.

*Match* - A contest to declare a winner between two or more opponents or teams.

*Official* - Designated leader whose responsibilities are to enforce the rules and regulations of the sport.

*Protest* - A complaint by an individual or team in a tournament regarding a rule interpretation.

*Round* - Completion of matches when all teams have played once or advanced with a bye. The last three rounds are called the finals (2 teams), semifinals (4 teams) and quarter finals (8 teams). In a round robin, it is when each team has played each other once.

*Seeding* - The placement of teams or individuals in different brackets so that those with superior records do not meet in the early rounds of a tournament.

*Tie Breaker* - Means for determining a winner after the regulation event has ended in a tie.

*Upset* - An unexpected loss by a favored team.

*Versus or vs.* - Term used to describe one team playing another.

*Winners Bracket* - Teams in a tournament with no losses.

*Losers Bracket* - Teams in a consolation or double elimination tournament who have lost at least one game.

NOTE: Besides these terms, most sports have a special vocabulary or jargon - for example, "scratch" in billiards or golf.